The European Union and Regional Integration in East Africa

This book examines European countries' engagement in promoting regional integration in the East African Community (EAC). In addition to their usage of the European Union (EU), states employ other bilateral initiatives to channel their regional aid to the EAC. The book explores differing national interests and the decisions to engage with the EAC, both multilaterally via the EU and through their other bilateral channels.

In addition to analysing states' interests, the book goes further, to examine how lack of coordination of those European initiatives creates various challenges in the EAC. It is shown how EAC bureaucrats have to engage separately with the EU and its member states in their different channels, thus experiencing challenges in different stages of their aid project cycles, for instance in the identification, implementation and reporting phases.

This book will be an excellent resource for researchers and practitioners focusing on the topics of European promotion of regional integration, development aid, African and European regional integration processes, as well as foreign policy analysis.

Harrison Kalunga Mwilima is an independent lecturer, consultant and journalist focusing on a sustainable relationship between Europe and Africa. He has lectured at the Berlin School of Economics and Law, Freie Universität Berlin and the European Institute (CIFE). He has written articles and opinion pieces for the German international broadcaster, the *Deutsche Welle* (DW), and advised different companies and organisations on various aspects of Europe–Africa relations.

Routledge Contemporary Africa

Combatants in African Conflicts
Professionals, Praetorians, Militias, Insurgents, and Mercenaries
Simon David Taylor

Popular Protest, Political Opportunities, and Change in Africa
Edited by Edalina Rodrigues Sanches

The Failure of the International Criminal Court in Africa
Decolonising Global Justice
Everisto Benyera

African Identities and International Politics
Frank Aragbonfoh Abumere

Quality Assessment and Enhancement in Higher Education in Africa
Edited by Peter Neema-Abooki

Media Ownership in Africa in the Digital Age
Challenges, Continuity and Change
Edited by Winston Mano and Loubna El Mkaouar

Policing and the Rule of Law in Sub-Saharan Africa
Edited by Oluwagbenga Michael Akinlabi

Tonga Livelihoods in Rural Zimbabwe
Edited by Kirk Helliker and Joshua Matanzima

Women Writers of the *New* African Diaspora
Transnational Negotiations and Female Agency
Pauline Ada Uwakweh

Africa-EU Relations and the African Continental Free Trade Area
Edited by Samuel Ojo Oloruntoba, Christopher Changwe Nshimbi and Leon Mwamba Tshimpaka

For more information about this series, please visit: https://www.routledge.com/ Routledge-Contemporary-Africa/book-series/RCAFR

The European Union and Regional Integration in East Africa

Collective and Individual State Priorities Compared

Harrison Kalunga Mwilima

LONDON AND NEW YORK

First published 2024
by Routledge
4 Park Square, Milton Park, Abingdon, Oxon OX14 4RN

and by Routledge
605 Third Avenue, New York, NY 10158

Routledge is an imprint of the Taylor & Francis Group, an informa business

British Library Cataloguing-in-Publication Data
A catalogue record for this book is available from the British Library

ISBN: 9781032268385 (hbk)
ISBN: 9781032268378 (pbk)
ISBN: 9781003290155 (ebk)

DOI: 10.4324/9781003290155

Typeset in Times New Roman
by Deanta Global Publishing Services, Chennai, India

To all who contribute to African regional Integration processes and ensure that African countries are becoming self-sufficient in financing their integration goals and agendas.

Contents

Tables

Abbreviations and Acronyms

AAMS	Association of African and Malagasy States
ACP	African Caribbean and Pacific
AfCFTA	African Continental Free Trade Area
AFD	*Agence française de développement*
AU	African Union
AUBP	African Union Border Programme
CET	Common External Tariff
COMESA	Common Market for Eastern and Southern Africa
DAC	Development Assistance Committee
DFID	Department for International Development
EAC	East African Community
EACSO	East African Common Service Organisation
EAHC	East African High Commission
EACJ	East African Court of Justice
EALA	East African Legislative Assembly
EAMS	East African Monitoring System
EA-SA-IO	Eastern Africa, Southern Africa and the Indian Ocean
EBA	Everything But Arms
ECCAS	Economic Community of Central African States
ECOWAS	Economic Community of West African States
EDF	European Development Fund
EIB	European Investment Bank
EPA	Economic Partnership Agreement
EU	European Union
FTA	Free Trade Area
GIZ	*Deutsche Gesellschaft für Internationale Zusammenarbeit*
GSP	General System of Preferences
IBM	Integrated Border Management
IMF	International Monetary Fund
KfW	*Kreditanstalt für Wiederaufbau*
LDCs	Least Development Countries
LVBC	Lake Victoria Basin Commission
MoU	Memorandum of Understanding

NBS	National Bureau of Standards
NGOs	Non-Governmental Organisations
Non-LDCs	Non-Least Developed Countries
NTBs	Non-Tariff Barriers
OACPS	Organisation of African, Caribbean and Pacific States
OECD	Organization for Economic Cooperation and Development
OCTs	Overseas Countries and Territories
OSBP	One Stop Border Post
PTA	Preferential Trade Area
PTB	*Physikalisch-Technische Bundesanstalt*
REPAs	Regional Economic Partnership Agreements
SADC	Southern Africa Development Community
Stabex	Stabilization Export Earnings
TMEA	TradeMark East Africa
UK	United Kingdom
UNCTAD	United Nations Conference on Trade and Development
WB	World Bank

Preface

In 2012 I visited the EAC headquarters in Arusha, Tanzania, and within the compound, I saw a smaller side house which raised my interest. When I asked about the presence of that house close to the EAC building, I was told that it was a former state house used to host member states' presidents when they visited the EAC; however, it is no longer used for that purpose. It changed its function and became an office for Germany's development agency, the GIZ. Having heard that, I left the EAC wondering why there is an office of a national development agency inside the EAC compound. Further research revealed to me that donor involvement in the EAC is quite common. I found out that while Germany was actively involved in supporting integration process, the EU and its other member states were also doing the same. That became even more puzzling for me; why would states support the EAC multilaterally via the EU as well as via their other bilateral channels? Figuring out that puzzle became the topic of my PhD dissertation starting from October 2013 all the way through to February 2017.

The main focus of the PhD dissertation was on why states chose both multilateral and bilateral channels to support regionalism. However, during the field research in East African countries in 2015, some of the interviewees raised some challenges related to the lack of European regional aid coordination. Although that was not the focus of my PhD question, it became clear that at some point I would need to address those challenges faced by EAC bureaucrats in dealing with the EU and its member states in their different channels. That was one of the major aims for seeking to write this book. As you will see, Part III of the book addresses the effects of differentiated European initiatives in the EAC. While the first two parts of the book deal with the same questions as in the PhD dissertation, the analysis goes further to include current empirical developments that occurred in recent years since the dissertation was submitted to the Freie Universität Berlin in 2017.

This book, however, can be seen as the peak of a long journey I have been undergoing over many years now. The topic of Europe–Africa relations in its various aspects has been my major focus since during my master's thesis and before. By then, interested in what the EAC could learn from the EU in its plans for monetary union, I generally became interested in European integration process after observing that the EAC was taking steps towards economic integration similar to those the EU started in the 1950s. As such, I saw the EU as an example from which we could learn and avoid some of its mistakes in order to achieve a successful integration that fit the East African context. After I finished my PhD studies in 2017, I decided to expand my interests beyond regionalism processes to focus on a sustainable relationship between Europe and Africa. Towards that end, I worked as an independent lecturer, consultant and journalist by engaging in teaching, advising and writing reports and opinion pieces focusing on different aspects of Europe–Africa relations. As you read this book, see it as my long journey that reflects my deep interests in Europe–Africa relations in their various aspects.

Acknowledgements

Some of the findings of this book are based on research for the PhD dissertation I submitted in February 2017 to the Freie Universität Berlin, Germany. For this, I wish to express my sincere gratitude to my principal supervisor Professor Tanja Börzel, who diligently monitored and made valuable comments at every stage of my work. I would also like to thank Professor Christof Hartman, who became my second supervisor. I am also grateful for the financial support I received from the German Research Foundation (DFG) through the doctoral grant of the *Kollegforschergruppe* (KFG) "The Transformative Power of Europe" at the Freie Universität Berlin.

For encouragement to further develop my dissertation into a book, I thank Professor José Magone, who always reminded me of the potential of the topic. I would like to thank the anonymous reviewers who commented on my book proposal and sent me their valuable feedback, which has been very useful towards realising this book.

Thanks also to Commissioning Editor Helena Hurd, who accompanied this book from the beginning to the end with lots of patience. I want to thank the Editorial Assistants Ella McFarlane, Katerina Lade and Rosie Anderson for having been always there to respond to my queries. I also thank very much the Production Editor Rachael Panthier for overseeing the production of the book, as well as Project Manager Sanjeevi Nagarajan for ensuring the final production process was smooth and swift.

I am extremely grateful to my wife Nora and our children Hanno, Mara and Malte for their unconditional love and support. They kept up with my busy schedule of writing the book while also doing my other daily works. And of course, my thanks also go to my parents, siblings and mother-in-law who have all been very supportive throughout the writing process.

Finally, since it is not possible to mention everyone here, I sincerely thank all those who assisted me in one way or the other in the course of writing this book.

1 Introduction

Promotion of regional integration is one of the major European Union (EU) external policies in its relations with other regions around the world. Javier Solana, the former High Representative for the Common Foreign and Security Policy of the EU, claimed in his undated speech that from 2005 onwards, the EU needed to take more responsibility on the international stage, suggesting regionalism promotion as one of the major ways to do so. Emphasising how such a policy fits into the EU's unique identity, he said:

> in Europe we have learned the hard way that sustainable peace and security require regional co-operation and integration ... That is why supporting regional co-operation is such a 'growth area' in our efforts. The African Union, Mercosur, Asean: these are all examples of strengthening regional regimes, explicitly taking their inspiration from the EU. We are deepening our relations with these other regional players and, where possible and relevant, we are giving our support for their further development.
>
> (Solana, n.d.)

Such aspirations resulted in numerous studies focusing on the EU's promotion of regional integration around the globe. For instance, in analysing the motivations for pursuing such a policy, scholars have regarded the EU as a rational actor going after its own interests but also as a normative actor doing what it perceives as the right thing to do (Börzel and Risse 2009; 2012; Farrell 2007; Lenz and Burilkov 2016).

Literature that has taken a rational approach has identified various interests which can be pursued by the EU through promoting regional integration. Economic interests, for instance, are regarded as one of the EU's major priorities and it pursues those by supporting economic liberalisation so that countries can remove external barriers to trade at the regional level (Hurt 2012; Storey 2006; Langan 2012). The EU can also use the external policy of promoting regional integration as a strategy to support stability in other parts of the world at the regional level, thereby preventing negative externalities from those regions, such as migration flow (Young 2004:422). The EU is

DOI: 10.4324/9781003290155-1

also interested in seeking power in the global arena as an international actor (Duchene 1972; Manners 2002; Nicolaidis and Howse 2002); thus, fostering regionalism can also be regarded as a rational act to attain more influence in different regions. As a means of pursuing those different interests while promoting regionalism, the EU can use various instruments, such as provision of technical and financial assistance in combination with conditionality in order to manipulate targeted actors to comply with EU's demands (Börzel and Risse 2009; 2012).

The literature that has adopted a normative approach, on the other hand, regards regional integration as an EU norm resulting from its own experience. As a regional organisation itself, the EU has managed to promote peace and facilitate economic cooperation in Europe after the disasters of the Second World War (Farrell 2007:302). In this regard, the EU aims to promote regional integration abroad due to the belief that it is the best way for neighbouring countries to address issues of common interest (Bicchi 2006:287). Furthermore, regionalism support is regarded as a distinct EU norm that has become part of its foreign policy towards other parts of the world in addition to other universal norms, such as promotion of democracy, human rights, good governance and rule of law (Lucarelli and Manners 2006; Manners 2002; Elgström 2006). Through that, the EU can also export its own model of integration, which it believes represents best practices to be emulated and promoted (Farrell 2007; Nicolaidis and Howse 2002; Bicchi 2006). As such, support of regional integration also becomes part of the EU's international identity, which makes the bloc different from other actors in the world (Manners and Whitman 1998; 2003; Diez 2005; Scheipers and Sicurelli 2007). These different ideational goals of pursuing norms and identity lead the EU to regard regionalism promotion as the best thing to do in its engagement with other regions around the world.

Surprisingly, the above-mentioned studies have all paid attention to the EU without taking into consideration the role of member states in promoting regional integration abroad. Although states delegated power to the EU to run a common European development policy that allows for promotion of regional integration, they also left the possibility of pursuing their national development policies. The process of Europeanisation on how the EU affects its member states (Börzel and Risse 2007:485) has only occurred to a modest degree in the area of development policy due to countries' preferences in maintaining their own bilateral development initiatives. The resistance of states to Europeanise their development aid policies is attributed to various factors, such as established cultural and normative structures, as well as existing differences among member states on their preferences towards development policies (Orbie and Carbone 2016). In that sense, EU member states can also adopt their own national development policies that also focus on promoting regional integration; however, less is known about states' initiatives towards other regional organisations. This book covers that literature gap by focusing on the case of the East African Community (EAC), whereby both the EU and its member states are involved in supporting its integration process.

The Case of East African Community

The EAC is a regional organisation that was revived in 2000 and its partner states include seven countries: Burundi, Democratic Republic of the Congo, Kenya, Rwanda, South Sudan, Tanzania and Uganda. Kenya, Tanzania and Uganda are the founding members, whereas Burundi and Rwanda joined the EAC in 2007. South Sudan became a full member in 2016 and the Democratic Republic of Congo in 2022.[1] The EAC established its customs union in 2005 and a common market in 2010. In 2013, the EAC partner states signed the protocol to establish a monetary union, which was expected to be in operation within ten years. When currency union is achieved, the EAC's remaining goal would be the attainment of a political federation. As one of the most ambitious regional organisations in Africa, European donor countries have been actively involved in supporting the EAC integration process not only multilaterally via the EU, but also through their other bilateral channels. Furthermore, some of the EU member states have colonial ties with EAC countries and such historical experiences also impacted earlier integration processes in the region.

During the colonial period, the region of East Africa was divided between two colonial powers: Germany and Britain. There was German East Africa which consisted of Tanganyika (the current Tanzanian mainland), Rwanda and Burundi, and British East Africa involving Kenya, Uganda and Zanzibar (the current Tanzanian island). After the First World War, when Germany lost all its colonies in 1919, Tanganyika was entrusted to the British, and Rwanda and Burundi to Belgium. The British incorporated Tanganyika with its other colonies, Kenya and Uganda, to form the foundation of integration for its colonial and imperial interests by establishing a customs union and harmonising the commercial laws of the three territories (di Delupis 1969:21). In 1948, the colonial government introduced an organisational framework known as the East African High Commission (EAHC) to manage common services in the region. The EAHC had to operate the East African Railways and Harbours, the East African Posts and Telegraph, the mechanism for revenue allocation, the East African Income Tax Management and the Makerere College (Adar and Ngunyi 1992:397). The activities of the EAHC favoured Kenya's economy more than Tanganyika and Uganda (ibid.: 398). In 1961, since the

---

1 Analysis of the EAC member states in this book will mainly focus on the five longer-established partner states of Burundi, Kenya, Rwanda, Tanzania and Uganda. The new member states, Democratic Republic of Congo and South Sudan, were not part of the EAC when the bloc negotiated earlier cooperation agreements with the EU.

East African countries were soon to become independent, the EAHC had to be replaced with the East African Common Service Organization (EACSO) (di Delupis 1969:42). The new EACSO, like the EAHC, continued to favour Kenya's economy over that of Tanganyika and Uganda (van Zwanenberg and King 1975:246.). The East African nationalist leaders were not satisfied with the dominance of Kenya's economy in the region; therefore, they dissolved the EACSO in 1966.

One year later, in 1967, the three independent countries Tanzania,[2] Kenya and Uganda signed the Treaty for East African Cooperation to further pursue the integration process. This time the partner states wanted to resolve their differences; therefore, some critical issues related to cooperation for mutual advantage were emphasised in the treaty (Hazlewood 1985:174). However, even in the new institution inequality persisted as Kenya continued to dominate trade in the EAC. Beyond the inequality between countries, there were also ideological differences between the leaders. Tanzania and Uganda adopted socialist policies while Kenya continued with capitalism. Later in 1971, Idi Amin staged a military coup in Uganda and became the president. The Tanzanian President Julius Nyerere refused to recognise Idi Amin. This situation further escalated the problems in the EAC, leading to its collapse in 1977.

After a long period, the three original member states, Tanzania, Kenya and Uganda, revived the integration process and signed the treaty to establish the EAC in 1999, which entered into force in 2000. Article 5, Section 2 of the Treaty for the Establishment of the EAC identifies the integration objectives of the Community starting from the customs union, followed by a common market, monetary union and ultimately a political federation. As mentioned earlier, the first two objectives are currently in full swing; however, there are still some challenges related to non-tariff barriers and the existence of a list of sensitive products that continue to undermine the free movement of goods and services as enshrined in the EAC customs union and common market protocols. Having achieved full economic integration, especially after adopting a currency union, the remaining goal of the EAC will be to finally achieve political federation. Such ambitious targets of the EAC, especially as the only African regional organisation intending to achieve political federation, pique donor countries' interest in supporting its integration process. That, in connection to historical linkages of its partner states with some of the EU countries, makes the EAC a "typical case" (Gerring and Seawright 2007:91), which can be used to study European countries' initiatives to promote regional integration abroad.

Beyond supporting the EAC multilaterally via the EU, states have employed three main bilateral channels in their engagement with the bloc, including using their own bilateral institutions, a non-profit company or contributing to the EAC Partnership Fund. The use of bilateral institutions

2 Tanganyika united with Zanzibar in 1964 to form Tanzania.

involves the implementation of supported projects through their national development agencies. On the other hand, donors can also channel their aid through a non-profit company called TradeMark East Africa (TMEA). The EAC Partnership Fund constitutes the contributions of donors to a basket fund, whereby the funds are made available for the EAC to finance its integration projects and activities. In the bilateral promotion of regional integration, eight EU member states, including Belgium, Denmark, Finland, France, Germany, the Netherlands, Ireland and Sweden have been supporting the EAC through those different bilateral channels. The United Kingdom (UK), which formally left the EU in 2020, was also one of the countries that supported the EAC, and its initiatives to support the bloc when it was still a member of the EU will also be analysed in this book. As shown in Table 1.1, Germany uses its bilateral institutions and contributed to the EAC Partnership Fund, but it does not use the non-profit company. The remaining donors use the non-profit company and contribute to the EAC Partnership Fund with the exception of Ireland and the Netherlands. The situation in the EAC and the variation in how the EU member states choose different strategies to promote regional integration raise three different questions that will be tackled in this book: (i) why do states promote regional integration multilaterally if they would rather do so bilaterally? (ii) Why do states choose different bilateral channels? And (iii) what are the effects of such differentiated European initiatives in the EAC?

Data Collection and Analysis

To respond to the three questions raised in this book, data has been collected from both primary and secondary sources. Primary data involve semi-structured interviews conducted in EAC countries with officials from five main

Table 1.1 EU Member States' Bilateral Promotion of Regional Integration

EU Member States	Bilateral Institution	Non-Profit Company	Partnership Fund
Belgium	0	1	1
Denmark	0	1	1
Finland	0	1	1
France	0	1	1
Germany	1	0	1
Ireland	0	1	0
Netherlands	0	1	0
Sweden	0	1	1
United Kingdom*	0	1	1

Source: Author's Own Compilation
* Although the United Kingdom left the EU in 2020, this book will analyse its regionalism support initiatives while it was still a member of the EU.

categories: (i) the EU member states and the EU working in the region; (ii) the EAC; (iii) TMEA; (iv) the national ministries of the EAC countries; and (v) experts of regional integration processes and donor involvement.[3] The analysis also relies on personal communications with EU member state and EAC officials. I also use primary data that involves documents from the EU and its member states as well as the EAC. That involves agreements, negotiations reports, development cooperation policy documents, foreign policy strategies and so forth.

Although the interviews and some of the primary documents were collected in 2015, the book goes further to include new developments on the topic. In analysing multilateral promotion of regional integration, for instance, I trace how European countries coordinated their development policy at the regional level, starting from 1957 when they signed the Treaty of Rome through different agreements and conventions that guided their relationship with Africa, Caribbean and Pacific (ACP) countries: the Yaoundé Convention (1964–1975), the Lomé Convention (1975–2000) and the Cotonou Agreement (2000–2020). Moreover, I further analyse the current ongoing negotiations for the post-Cotonou Agreement on how the EU and ACP countries intend to continue with their cooperation in three main areas of aid, trade and political dialogue. Analysis of bilateral promotion of regional integration also involves current empirical developments that occurred in recent times. As we will see, EU member states continued to support the EAC through their bilateral institutions and via the TMEA; however, in 2016 they stopped contributing to the Partnership Fund and preferred to finance projects on their own. In the analysis of effects of European initiatives to the EAC, it will be shown how the EU continued to partially coordinate some of its regional aid with that of its member states in their different bilateral channels.

Apart from primary data collected through interviews, personal communications and primary documents, this study also relies on a combination of literature from European integration, foreign policy analysis as well as development aid. In responding to the question of multilateral support of regionalism, European integration literature enables this study to examine how EU member states coordinated that policy at the EU level, leaving the possibility of pursuing their other bilateral channels. Foreign policy analysis approaches provide this study with the framework to analyse EU member states' preferences and national interests towards the EAC to explain why they chose different bilateral channels. Development aid literature provides concepts to assess the effects of European differentiated initiatives in the EAC, especially when they operate in an uncoordinated manner.

The use of all these primary and secondary data is employed as a means of triangulation – "aimed at corroborating the same finding" (Yin

3 Interviewees are not named in this book due to my promise of anonymity.

2014:120–121). In this sense, I employ a convergence of multiple sources of evidence whereby the findings are supported by more than a single piece of evidence (ibid.: 121). For instance, if an interviewee – say an official from a certain EU member state – claims that they follow a certain norm in their selection of a bilateral channel to support the EAC, then I will try to find out in that country's official policy documents or from the statements of other officials if that specific norm is indeed expressed.

Main Argument

The book makes three major arguments in responding to the three questions asked in this study. First, on the question of why states support regionalism multilaterally if they would rather do so bilaterally, I argue that multilateral promotion of regional integration is a result of powerful states influencing the coordination of a common European development policy at the EU level. However, those influential countries are divided into two major camps: "regionalists," which prefer EU policy to focus on former colonies, and "globalists," which support policy that focuses on poverty levels in the poorest countries. The division of powerful states into these two major camps led states to undergo a lowest-common-denominator bargaining style, thereby reaching a common development policy that does not satisfy all states. That has been happening in several negotiations which led to the signing of different agreements and conventions between the EU and ACP countries. As the policy originated in 1957 and has gone through various phases until the current era, it becomes more difficult for states to reject it, even when they are not satisfied with the common agreed position. In that way, they end up continuing with multilateral promotion of regional integration via the EU, despite their preferences to use other bilateral channels. As such, through bilateral channels, states can pursue their individual national preferences, whereas common European interests towards other regions can be secured through supporting regionalism multilaterally via the EU.

With regard to the second question, on why countries choose different channels, I argue that their choices depend on their national interests towards the EAC and their capacities to pursue them in the region. Choosing bilateral institutions to support integration also means having major interests in the region and capacity to act on them. Germany, as the only country which engages with the EAC through its own national development agency, is therefore argued to be highly interested in the regional organisation. That interest results mainly from Germany's internalisation of the regional integration promotion norm, its preferences to preserve a unique identity as an older partner of the EAC as well as its potential need to establish a strong relationship with a region in which some of its member states are its lost former colonies. On the selection of a non-profit company, it is argued that powerful states without strong interests in establishing a unique identity or without direct colonial linkages to the EAC countries, for instance France, are fine with the usage of the TMEA. Furthermore, all states, either powerful or small, are regarded as having chosen the non-profit company since they consider it as the best way to support the EAC and pursue their interests in the region. On contributing to the Partnership Fund, I maintain that donors get involved in the basket fund to mainly signal that they are concerned with aid coordination, and that is why they were contributing to it in addition to the other bilateral channels of their interests.

On the third question, on the effects of European engagement in the EAC, it is argued that lack of full coordination between the EU and its member states in their initiatives to support regional integration creates various challenges to EAC bureaucrats. Those challenges are experienced by bureaucrats especially when they have to engage separately with the EU and its member states in the different stages of their aid cycles, such as through identification, implementation and reporting phases. During the identification phase, for instance, bureaucrats have to interact with each and every donor when identifying new projects to be financed. The implementation phases are challenging when donors decide to execute their own projects, thus making it difficult for bureaucrats to have a clear overview on what is being done by each donor and how their activities are connected to the general goals of the EAC. During the reporting phase, challenges can occur when donors finance projects and do their own reports, thus making it difficult for the EAC bureaucrats to control the impact of donors' finances, especially when they do not go via EAC budget procedures. An additional question has also been posed on the effects of those states' bilateral initiatives on the EU especially on whether the bloc can be regarded as an aid-coordinating actor. In connection to that, it is shown how the EU is not regarded as a coordinating actor either by European officials working in the region or local bureaucrats, due to the lack of full coordination of those European initiatives in supporting the EAC.

Structure of the Book

This book is divided into three main parts based on the three questions that have been raised. The first part starts by explaining multilateral promotion of regional integration, the second examines states' selection of bilateral channels and the third analyses the effects of those European differentiated initiatives on the EAC. Each part has two chapters, with the first outlining a theoretical framework to explain the outcome, while the second provides an assessment of empirical evidence. The upcoming first part of the book starts by analysing how multilateral promotion of regional integration occurs through three main instruments of aid, trade and political dialogue. The chapter then introduces a modified intergovernmentalism theoretical framework that will explain how states have delegated their development policy at the EU level to allow for multilateral promotion of regional integration. In this sense, three stages of liberal intergovernmentalism, starting from national preference formation, followed by interstate bargaining and outcome, is linked to how states have delegated their development policy at the EU level. In the final stage of outcome, a theory of path dependence is introduced to show how past decisions of delegating the policy at EU level is expected to lead member states to continue supporting integration multilaterally despite their interests in using other bilateral channels. Having explained the theoretical framework, Chapter 3 dives into empirics to examine how countries have delegated that policy at EU level while still leaving the possibility of pursuing their own bilateral channels. The chapter is divided into four phases based on the agreements and conventions that were signed between the EU and ACP countries: from the Treaty of Rome to the expiration of the Yaoundé Convention (1957–1975), the Lomé Convention (1975–2000), the Cotonou Agreement (2000–2020) and the post-Cotonou Agreement. Within each of those phases it is shown how the formation of national preferences, interstate bargaining and outcome occurred, as proposed by the theory of liberal intergovernmentalism.

The second part of the book, on how states have chosen different bilateral channels, starts with Chapter 4 by introducing the theoretical framework, followed by Chapter 5 on empirical evidence. Chapter 4 introduces three foreign policy analysis approaches that are used to explain states' decisions, including power-, interest-, and norms/identity-based approaches. Different assumptions based on the theories are provided to determine why states would choose to engage with the EAC via bilateral institutions, a non-profit company or contributing to the Partnership Fund. The power-based approach mainly explains the decisions of powerful EU member states including France, Germany and the UK's involvement when it was still a member of the EU. The remaining interest and norms/identity-based approaches explain all EU member states' engaging with the EAC regardless of their power position and capacities in the region. After laying the theoretical framework, Chapter 5 explores how those theories explain the situation on the ground. The chapter discusses each of the bilateral channels while comparing how the three foreign policy approaches determine states' decisions.

The third part of the book on the effects of European initiatives to support regional integration in the EAC consists of Chapter 6, which explains the theoretical framework, followed by Chapter 7 on empirics. Chapter 6 starts by elucidating the concept of regional integration and defining the sectors that can typically be financed through regional aid, including regional economic integration, security, institutions, as well as provision of capacity-building to non-state actors and member states. The chapter also draws from development aid literature on donor coordination and aid proliferation to describe how lacking full coordination between the EU and its member states in their support of regional integration can affect EAC bureaucrats, especially in their engagement with all the donors in different stages of their aid cycle, including identification, implementation and reporting phases. Chapter 7 then moves on to the empirical situation, starting by analysing how European countries duplicate their aid in different regional sectors. This shows how lack of full coordination between the EU and its member states occurs while interacting with the EAC. Despite the EU's initiatives to partially coordinate some of its projects with those of its member states through, for instance, matching of projects and co-financing, challenges have been experienced by EAC bureaucrats due to interacting separately with each and every donor. Furthermore, the chapter also shows how member states' bilateral initiatives cause the EU to not be perceived as a coordinating actor in the region. Finally, Chapter 8 concludes the book by summarising major findings and highlighting the research and policy implications of the findings. Let us now move on to the first part of the book on multilateral promotion of regional integration, starting with the theoretical framework.

Part I

Multilateral Promotion of Regional Integration

2 Collective Interests and Regionalism Support

Promotion of regional integration at the EU level can be seen as an effort by member states to pursue collective interests towards other regional organisations, which is part and parcel of common European development policy, whereby states have delegated power to the EU to be able to support regionalism in other parts of the world. Through this, states can come up with a common position on how the EU, specifically the European Commission, can engage with other areas of interest to them. To elucidate this collective engagement of supporting regionalism, this chapter is divided into two main sections. The first section focuses on how multilateral promotion of regional integration by member states through the EU is implemented in the EAC. In the second section I introduce a modified intergovernmentalism theoretical framework that will be used to explain how states have delegated power to the EU so as to support regionalism but have retained the possibility of doing the same via other bilateral channels.

Multilateral Promotion of Integration

The EU's development policy of supporting regional integration in the EAC and ACP countries, in general, is guided by the Cotonou Agreement that was signed in 2000 in Cotonou, Benin, and was expected to end in 2020. On 15 April 2021, the post-Cotonou Agreement was initialled, but at the time of writing it has not been approved and ratified by ACP countries. In the meantime, the Cotonou Agreement that was supposed to end in 2020 has been prolonged, until the new pact enters into force (European Parliament 2022). The Cotonou Agreement and the current initialled pact outlines how the EU and ACP countries can cooperate in the three main areas of aid, trade and political dialogue. These areas are also used by the EU as instruments to support regional integration in the ACP countries. As we will see in this section, while aid is mainly used to finance integration activities, trade establishes commercial links with regional organisations, whereas political dialogue involves consultations at the regional level. These three instruments of aid, trade and political dialogue can have conditionality attached in order to

DOI: 10.4324/9781003290155-3

achieve European collective interests in the EAC and ACP regional groups in general.

Aid, as one of the major instruments used by the EU to support regionalism, mainly comes from the European Development Fund (EDF). Generally, the EDF is used by the EU to provide development assistance to ACP countries as well as Overseas Countries and Territories (OCTs). Part of that money can also be channelled to regional organisations in ACP countries in order to finance integration activities. In addition to the EDF, ACP countries and OCTs can also receive development aid through specific thematic development programmes financed under the EU budget. The EAC, as one of the regional organisations within the ACP group of countries, also receives the EDF and other funds via the EU budget. From the EDF budget between 2014 and 2020, the EAC received EUR 85 million from the EU to finance its integration projects (Regional Indicative Programme for EA-SA-IO 2014–2020). In addition, the EAC can receive extra funds for infrastructure, cross-regional facilities and technical cooperation facilities (ibid.:21). The EUR 85 million allocated to the EAC was earmarked to four different areas: (i) EUR 15 million was reserved for peace, security and stability with the objective of promoting democratic governance and combating terrorism, cross-border and transnational organised crime such as human trafficking, migrant smuggling, as well as trafficking of small arms and light weapons, wildlife and narcotics; (ii) EUR 45 million was allocated in regional economic integration to foster the implementation of the EAC common market as well as monitoring the customs union and common market protocols plus supporting industries and the private sector in facilitating trade in the region; (iii) EUR 20 million was earmarked in regional natural resource management mainly to support the integrated management and development of the shared water and fishery resources of the Lake Victoria Basin; and (iv) the remaining EUR 5 million was reserved for institutional capacity-building of the EAC Secretariat and other institutions to deliver effectively on their mandates (ibid.).

The trade instrument of regionalism support for ACP countries is implemented by the EU through a trade policy known as the Economic Partnership Agreements (EPAs). EPAs were introduced in the Cotonou Agreement and the policy was regarded as having the effect of facilitating regional integration in the ACP regional groups through trade with the EU at regional level (Article 37 of the Cotonou Agreement). In this sense, a reciprocal trade relationship was introduced, and ACP regional groups had to sign EPAs and agree to gradually open their markets for EU products if they wanted to continue exporting free of duty to EU countries. However, ACP countries that are "non-least developed countries" (non-LDCs) and did not agree to EPAs would lose their free access to EU markets and would export under the General System of Preferences (GSP) instead. Meanwhile, the "least developed countries" (LDCs) would continue to export duty-free and quota-free to the EU under the Everything But Arms (EBA) arrangement. EAC countries signed the interim

EPA as a regional bloc in 2007 during its initial negotiations with the EU. In the absence of that, Kenya, which was the only non-LDC in the region, would lose free-market access to the EU and export under the GSP, while the remaining LDCs (Tanzania, Uganda, Rwanda and Burundi) would continue to export duty-free and quota-free to the EU under the EBA arrangement. As signatories of the interim EPA, the EAC countries continued to export to the EU duty- and quota-free and negotiations continued towards obtaining a comprehensive EPA. Signing a regional comprehensive EPA would also mean that EAC countries as a bloc are required to open their markets gradually to EU products by 82.6% in 25 years (European Commission 2019). On 16 October 2014, the negotiations were finalised, and the implementation of the agreement waited for approval in accordance with the domestic procedures of each EAC country (European Commission 2014). On 1 September 2016, Kenya and Rwanda signed the regional EPA, but other EAC member states including Tanzania, Uganda and Burundi did not want to sign due, among other things, to fear that the free trade proposed through EPAs would lead to the destruction of local industries in their countries (Mwilima 2019). During the EAC Summit that took place on 27 February 2021, one of the major conclusions that was reached involved recognising the fact that not all EAC member states are in a position to sign, ratify and implement the EPA; therefore, those countries who wished to do so were allowed to further engage with the EU to start implementing the EU–EAC EPA under the principle of variable geometry (EAC 2021). Kenya decided to pursue this bilateral approach and on 17 February 2022, the EU and Kenya launched talks on an interim EPA (European Commission 2022a). Such differences, of some countries wanting to sign EPAs and others not, have been regarded by scholars as potentially undermining the integration process and go contrary to what was anticipated through the trade policy of EPAs as a means of facilitating regionalism through trading with the EU at regional level (Söderbaum 2013:30).

As an instrument to support regional integration, political dialogue requires the EU and the ACP regional groups to discuss issues of common challenges. Article 8 of the Cotonou Agreement identifies that dialogue should contribute to peace, security and stability and promote a stable and democratic political environment. To this end, the article further describes different areas on which political dialogue can focus, which include the arms trade, excessive military expenditure, drugs and organised crime. In Article 9, the agreement also refers to the essential elements within political dialogue constituting human rights, democratic principles, the rule of law and good governance. The Cotonou Agreement goes further, to introduce the possibility of sanctions when there is violation of those essential elements. This is referred to in Article 96 of the Agreement, where it is clearly stated that if political dialogue does not produce any results, then appropriate measures in accordance with international law will be taken. The instrument of political dialogue is regarded by scholars as enabling the EU to also pursue its security interests towards ACP countries and regions (Bagoyoko and Gibert 2009:792; Farrell 2013:114). The EU regards instability in African countries as having negative effects on European security, for instance through illegal migration and trafficking of arms, drugs and refugee flows (European Commission 2006:5). Some of the described areas in political dialogue clearly deal with these European perceived security threats coming from some African countries. Furthermore, the promotion of essential elements regarding human rights, democratic principles, the rule of law and good governance, is considered in the European Security Strategy as a means of dealing with security threats through fostering political stability (Council of the European Union 2003). By the same token, political dialogue has also been considered by other scholars as enabling the EU to promote its norms and values of democracy, human rights and good governance in other regions (Farrell 2013; Börzel and Risse 2009). In the case of the EAC, one of the major documented political dialogues between the bloc and the EU took place on 11 February 2015. The focus of the dialogue was mainly on peace and security in the region as well as the role of the EAC in promoting good governance, especially in election observation within its member states (EAC-EU Press Release 2015). Furthermore, sanctions have also been employed by the EU towards some members of the EAC when essential elements of human rights, democratic principles, the rule of law and good governance have been violated. This was the case in 2015, when the EU suspended its aid to Burundi due to the deteriorating political situation caused by the disputed presidential election (EAC 2022a). These financial sanctions were lifted in 2022 after Burundi had taken various measures to ensure peaceful political processes (ibid.).

This section shows that the promotion of regional integration multilaterally via the EU enables states to collectively use the three main instruments of aid, trade policy and political dialogue. These instruments can also be employed with other mechanisms, such as conditionality, to further pursue collective European interests. Conditionality, in the context of this book, is defined as the capability of an actor to induce negative and positive incentives in order to manipulate the decisions of the target actors (Börzel and Risse 2009; 2012). Through positive incentives, targeted actors could receive rewards such as financial and technical assistance, whereas negative incentives could constitute punishment in the form of sanctions (ibid.). Development aid is one of those instruments which can be used to instigate both positive and negative incentives. The funds which are used to support integration can be channelled to the regional organisations, and actors in those blocs would know if they complied to demands from the EU, in which case money would continue to flow into their organisations (positive incentive). On the other hand, aid can be withdrawn from those regional organisations if they don't comply with EU demands (negative incentive). The trade policy of EPAs is also used in combination with both positive and negative incentives. Those countries and regional groups which sign the EPA are rewarded with free access to EU markets (positive incentives), whereas those countries which have not signed the EPA and are non-LDCs, face tariffs when exporting to the EU (negative incentive). Political dialogue has also been applied, together with aid, in order to induce positive and negative incentives while facilitating compliance to different themes of concern. To that end, if ACP states and regions comply with the demands of the dialogue they then receive further aid (positive incentive), and if not, the aid can be suspended (negative incentive). Furthermore, if development aid is not enough, political dialogue can also be combined with losing access to the EU's market in order to enforce certain changes in ACP countries and regions. Despite the existence of all these instruments to pursue collective European interests, the question remains as to why states are interested in using extra bilateral channels to support integration. In the following section, I introduce a modified intergovernmentalism theoretical framework which will be used to explain that outcome.

Intergovernmentalism and Collective Regionalism Support

To examine why states have coordinated their development policy to allow the EU to promote regional integration, while also doing the same through other bilateral channels, it is necessary to explore decision-making processes at the EU level. An intergovernmentalism approach, with its focus on the importance of states in influencing decisions within the EU, provides an important framework within which to analyse that situation. The main argument of intergovernmentalism is, as the name suggests, that the EU's member governments play a strong role when it comes to decision-making at the regional level. Stanley Hoffmann, who first developed this assumption, was intrigued by the empirical developments of the 1960s in Europe, whereby the French government resisted the gradual transfer of sovereignty to the European Community in order to ensure that decision-making powers regarding major issues remain in the hands of member states (Hoffmann 1966).

In the 1990s, when European integration progressed further, with the implementation of single market and the signing of the Maastricht Treaty, intergovernmentalism took a different turn in explaining these new developments. Andrew Moravcsik proposed a new model which he called liberal intergovernmentalism to explain the influence of powerful EU member states in facilitating such rapid integration progress (Moravcsik 1993; 1995; 1998). Liberal intergovernmentalism theoretical framework suggested three different steps in how states make decisions at the EU level, starting with national preference formation, followed by interstate bargaining and, later, outcome (ibid.). At the first stage, of national preference formation, Moravcsik used a liberal theory to show how government leaders take into consideration the demands of their domestic groups when formulating their interests towards the EU. The second stage, of interstate bargaining, is where the intergovernmental model of EU-level bargaining is used to show how national governments engage in negotiations in order to pursue their formulated national preferences. Finally, in the last stage, of outcome, a rational choice theory is employed to explain adoption of institutional choice at the EU level in order to ensure credible commitments among states. Institutional choice, in that sense, could either involve pooling of sovereignty – whereby decision-making power remains at state level, for instance through qualified majority voting – or delegation of sovereignty to the EU institutions.

In the context of regionalism support, states' institutional choice involved delegation of power to the EU, but at the same time they maintained the possibility of employing other bilateral channels. As explained earlier, promotion of regional integration is part of the EU's common development policy towards ACP countries. In this regard, the three-stage model of liberal intergovernmentalism is used to explain how such delegation of power has occurred towards the policy. For this reason, the section starts by examining national preference formation in order to assess states' interests when coordinating development policy at the EU level. Afterwards, I move on to analyse how interstate bargaining is expected to take place and wind up with the outcome section on institutional choice. As you will see at the final stage of outcome, the intergovernmentalism framework is modified through combining the theory of path dependence to explain states' multilateral promotion of regional integration, despite their interests in using other bilateral channels.

National Preferences

The first step in coordinating development policy which allows for multilateral promotion of regional integration begins with national preference formation. States need to have an interest in coordinating that policy at the EU level. Such interests, which constitute either economic or geopolitical interests, result mainly from domestic groups that influence states' apparatus (Moravcsik 1998:24). In defining further those two major national interests, Moravcsik argues that "geopolitical interests reflect perceived threats to national sovereignty or territorial integrity, whether military or ideological," whereas "economic interests reflect the imperatives induced by interdependence and, in particular, the large exogenous increase in opportunities for profitable cross-border trade and capital movement" (ibid.:26).

As shown in the previous section, the geopolitical interests of European countries towards Africa mainly involve promotion of political stability to avoid negative externalities, such as illegal migration, whereas economic interests constitute accessing markets for trade and investments. Furthermore, interest in maintaining colonial ties is a major preference for some European countries towards their former colonies in Africa. Former colonial powers may be concerned with the security of their former colonies and may also have economic interests due to the strong ties established during the colonial period. Powerful EU countries which had colonies are able to use their influence within the EU to coordinate policy at the regional level that might target their former colonies.

When states coordinated European common development policy to facilitate their multilateral promotion of regional integration, the preference of maintaining colonial ties played a strong role. Research shows that national preferences on development policy coordination, especially towards African countries, have been typically divided into two major camps based on states' colonial histories. On the one hand, countries dubbed as regionalists preferred European development policy to focus mainly on former colonies. On the other hand, a globalist camp of states favoured the policy of generally focusing on poor countries. The regionalist camp was led by France with support from Belgium, Portugal and Spain, whereas the globalist position was spearheaded by Germany and the UK, with further backing from the Netherlands and the Scandinavian countries (Carbone 2007; Ravenhill 1985:42; Mailafia 1997:63; Frisch 2013:111). It is surprising to see a country with a strong colonial history such as the UK in the globalist camp rather than the regionalist camp, along with other former colonial powers. With regard to the UK, it can be argued that it became a globalist due to the nature of its colonies which are spread across the African continent.[1] Furthermore, Germany may have chosen a globalist position due to the loss of its colonies in 1919 after being defeated in the First World War.[2] France, on the other hand, preferred a regionalist position due to the fact that most of its former colonies are mainly concentrated in West Africa.[3]

Various assumptions about national preferences can be made based on states' colonial histories and the camps they preferred to support while coordinating European development policy. First, those states without colonial ties are less likely to be interested in coordinating policy at the EU level, and, if they have a preference, will choose a globalist position. On the other hand, states which lost their colonies, or have their former colonies spread across many regions, are more likely to prefer a globalist approach. Finally, EU

---

1 British former colonies are spread in southern, western, eastern and northern Africa. Some examples include the modern countries of South Africa, Zambia, Botswana, Malawi, Zimbabwe and Lesotho (in southern Africa); Ghana, Nigeria, Gambia and Sierra Leone (in western Africa); Kenya and Uganda (in eastern Africa) and Egypt and Sudan (in northern Africa).

2 Later, in Chapter 5, it will be argued that Germany might be interested in reactivating contacts with its lost colonies of the modern countries of Burundi, Rwanda and the Tanzanian mainland, which were previously known as German East Africa. Being active in supporting integration in the EAC could be a means for Germany to activate a strong partnership with the regional organisation of which three of its former colonies are members. The remaining three German colonies of Cameroon, Namibia and Togo are spread across central, southern and western Africa respectively.

3 French West Africa involved the modern countries of Mauritania, Senegal, Mali, Guinea, Ivory Coast, Burkina Faso, Benin and Niger. Though France had colonies in other parts of Africa, such as Algeria, Tunisia and Morocco (in northern Africa), Djibouti (in eastern Africa), Madagascar (in southern Africa) and Central Africa Republic, Chad and the Republic of Congo (in Central Africa), French West Africa was concentrated in a specific region under one administrative body.

countries which have their former colonies concentrated in a specific region are likely to pursue a regionalist approach. Once states have developed their national preferences towards coordinating development policy with regard to the three instruments of supporting regionalism, the second stage is interstate bargaining with other members of the EU.

Interstate Bargaining

The second stage, of interstate bargaining, is where states bring their national preferences to the negotiating table at the regional level. In this sense, they put forward their proposals on how they want to coordinate European development policy towards ACP countries. Their preferences on aid, trade and political dialogue are then negotiated and one position in each of these instruments is chosen to be the common European development policy towards ACP countries. At this stage Moravcsik applies intergovernmental bargaining theory to show how powerful EU member states such as France, Germany and the former EU member country of the UK can use their influence and bargaining power to facilitate adoption of treaties and different common European policies (Moravcsik 1998:60–67).

In explaining further interstate bargaining processes within the EU, Moravcsik draws from game theory to show how powerful states with certain preferences towards a specific regional agreement can use concessions and compromises to achieve their goals, whereas small countries can engage in issue linkage or be offered side payments to accept a certain position in the agreements (ibid.). Issue linkages can occur when negotiators link "unrelated or only loosely-related issues in order to gain increased leverage in negotiation" (Wallace 1976:164). In this sense, negotiators can try to add or subtract various unrelated issues in the negotiation to achieve a certain agreement (Sebenius 1983). Issue linkages can also take the form of side payments, which can involve financial assistance to the party that might oppose the agreement or supporting them in other issue areas of their interests (Mayer 1988:177–179). Moravcsik (1991:25–26) also argues that intergovernmental bargaining in the EU can converge towards the lowest common denominator of powerful states, and thus they have to accept decisions on major issues that they do not favour.

The use of concessions and compromises, as well as engagement in issue linkages and side payments, can also be employed during the negotiations towards coordinating development policy that allows for multilateral promotion of regional integration. In this regard, two major assumptions can be developed on how interstate bargaining would take place when agreeing on policy and cooperation with ACP countries on the three instruments of aid, trade and political dialogue. First, the more intensely a powerful state prefers a certain position with regard to the policy of promoting regional integration multilaterally, the greater its incentive to offer concessions and compromises.

Second, small states are more likely to be offered side payments or to engage in issue linkages in their support of powerful states' positions towards coordinating the policy to promote regional integration multilaterally. As shown earlier, states' preferences towards Africa, and ACP countries in general, are mainly influenced by colonial linkages. Therefore, if, say, regionalist countries are more interested in a certain position, then France, who leads the camp, would offer more concessions and compromises as well as engage in side payments towards small states.

Outcome

After interstate bargaining, states enter the third and final stage, of outcome, in order to achieve a regional agreement. As explained earlier, this stage is where they decide about institutional choice on whether to delegate or pool decision-making power to EU institutions. In the case of regionalism support, states decided to delegate power to the EU to be able to use aid, trade and political dialogue in its promotion of integration. At the same time, they also retain the possibility of doing the same thing via other bilateral channels. In this section, I consider the role of path dependence to partly explain countries' continued multilateral participation even when they are interested in using other bilateral channels.

Path dependence explains how decisions made in the past may have an influence on future decisions. As Page (2006:89) suggests, "the path of previous outcomes matters." This can be the case in the EU's development policy towards ACP countries which also allows for multilateral promotion of regional integration. The policy was first established in 1957 when European countries were signing the Treaty of Rome to establish the European Economic Community (EEC). As a consequence, such long relationships with the ACP countries may have created a link that is difficult to break in the current era, even when states may not be satisfied with the common position at the EU level. It was argued earlier that states' preferences towards ACP countries typically divide along colonial linkages, with countries preferring either a regionalist or globalist position. Therefore, intergovernmental bargaining in the EU can converge towards the lowest common denominator of powerful states, meaning that countries may have to accept a common position that they may not favour. Although such a situation is likely to occur while coordinating common development policy, states would still prefer to engage with the ACP regions multilaterally via the EU, even when they are interested in using other bilateral channels. Connecting such an outcome with the theory of path dependence, it is assumed that even when a common position at EU level does not satisfy all member states, countries are still likely to continue using the multilateral channel to promote regional integration due to the difficulties of rejecting the previous path.

The continuation of EU development policy into the present era also enables member states to pursue common European interests, such as economic and security goals, or seek to promote norms towards ACP countries. As shown in the previous section, the EU's support of regionalism involves the three different instruments of aid, trade and political dialogue, which can be combined with conditionality in order to pursue common European interests. In this sense, it can further be assumed that states prefer to support regionalism at a multilateral level as a means of securing collective European interests; and when they have individual national interests in a specific region, they will engage with those regional organisations via other bilateral channels. Having explained the theoretical framework, the following chapter assesses the empirical situation.

3 Coordinating Multilateral Regionalism Support

Now we come to the analysis of how EU member states coordinated their development policy to allow for multilateral promotion of regional integration. In this chapter, I trace how that coordination evolved over time based on the agreements and conventions which were signed between the EU and ACP countries. To that end, the chapter is divided into four phases: from the Treaty of Rome to the expiration of the Yaoundé Convention (1957–1975), the Lomé Convention (1975–2000), the Cotonou Agreement (2000–2020) and the post-Cotonou Agreement. In each of those four phases it will be examined how the EU and ACP countries decided to cooperate in the three major areas of aid, trade and political dialogue. To analyse why states promote regional integration multilaterally despite their interest in doing so via bilateral channels, a modified intergovernmentalism theoretical framework has been selected. Therefore, in each of those four phases it will be examined how states formed their preferences and were involved in interstate bargaining leading to the outcome of coordinating policy. In terms of data collection and analysis, the chapter relies mainly on primary literature by scholars and people with direct knowledge of internal negotiations on how states coordinated EU development policy towards ACP countries in different phases.

From the Treaty of Rome to the Expiration of the Yaoundé Convention (1957–1975)

During the early establishment of European integration, some states wanted to maintain relationships with their African colonies within the framework of the EEC, especially in the areas of aid and trade agreements. Consequently, the Treaty of Rome, which established the EEC, included a section on association countries which constituted the EEC countries' colonies that would receive aid and trade preferential treatment.[1] These policies continued, even when the

---

1 These countries and territories were listed in Annex IV of the Treaty of Rome and included: (i) French West Africa: Senegal, the French Sudan (Mali), Guinea, the Ivory Coast, Dahomey (Benin), Mauritania, Niger and Upper Volta (Burkina Faso); (ii) French Equatorial Africa, which

DOI: 10.4324/9781003290155-4

colonies attained independence through the signing of the Yaoundé I and II Conventions, until 1975. In this first phase, we will see how French preferences were influential in establishing the policy. The analysis of the first phase will confirm the assumptions raised in the previous chapter on how France, which had colonies concentrated in West Africa, supported the regionalist position, while being supported by other small colonial powers. On the other hand, Germany, which lost its colonies, supported a globalist stance and was backed by other countries which had no interests in maintaining colonial ties. Furthermore, in terms of interstate bargaining, the first phase confirms the assumption that the more strongly a state prefers an agreement, the more likely it is to make concessions and compromises and fulfil the expectation that small states will likely engage in issue linkages in their support of powerful countries' positions. This will be shown by how France made concessions and compromises towards West Germany, while small colonial powers such as Belgium and Italy supported the French position by engaging in issue linkages.

The Treaty of Rome and the Emergence of Association

The origin of EU development policy towards African countries can be traced back to the Treaty of Rome which was signed in 1957. The Treaty established the EEC among six countries: Belgium, France, Italy, Luxembourg, the Netherlands and West Germany. It proposed the formation of a customs union and the creation of a common market among the six EEC member states. The customs union meant that all third countries exporting to the EEC had to pay a Common External Tariff (CET). However, some of the EEC countries still had colonies in other parts of the world. France, for instance, was engaged in a common market with its colonies and the currency used in the colonies – the *Communauté Financière Africaine* (CFA) franc – was closely linked to the French franc (Migani 2013:16). In such a situation, France had to either abandon its common market with the colonies or include them in the new EEC framework. France chose the latter, and during the common market negotiations, the French government proposed the idea of incorporating the colonial territories into a form of association in the EEC framework and declared the issue to be an essential condition for its signing of the treaty (Mailafia 1997:40).

---

included the Middle Congo (Republic of Congo), Ubangi-Shari (Central African Republic), Chad and Gabon; (iii) St. Pierre and Miquelon, the Comoro Archipelago, Madagascar and dependencies, New Macedonia and dependencies, the French Somali coast, the French settlement in Oceana, the Southern and Antarctic Territories; (iv) the autonomous Republic of Togoland; (v) the French Trusteeship Territory in the Cameroons; (vi) the Belgian Congo and Ruanda-Urundi; (vii) the trusteeship territory of Somaliland under Italian administration; (viii) Netherlands New Guinea.

In the negotiation of the Treaty of Rome, the French government also wanted other European countries to share the financial burden of supporting its colonies. France was then fighting independent wars in Indochina and Algeria and was also financing development projects in colonies as a means of its economic recovery after the Second World War; therefore, the French government needed developmental support of its colonies from other EEC countries (ibid.:40–43). As a result, France wanted the Treaty to establish the EDF to which other European countries would contribute and share the costs of financing overseas colonies' activities (Migani 2013:16).

Other European countries, especially West Germany and the Netherlands, were against French demands for this association with regard to the colonies. For other member states, such as Belgium, Italy and Luxembourg, the issue was not of great importance (Twitchett 1978:12–15; Milward 1992:219–220). Although Italy was entrusted to administer former Italian Somaliland, while Belgium was responsible for the Congo and the Trust Territories of Rwanda and Burundi, they did not find it necessary to extend preferential treatment to their colonies during the negotiation of the Treaty; however, Belgium was more sympathetic to France's "Eur-African" aspirations (Ravenhill 1985:50). Italy, on the other hand, though it did not have any preferences, decided to opportunistically support the French position, despite the fact that it was concerned about the impact the association would have on its agricultural sector as well as the contribution it would have to make to the EDF (Carbone 2007:170). This behaviour of the small EU member states can be described as attempts at issue linkages; thus countries such as Belgium and Italy supported the French position, connecting that support to other issues such as sympathy or other future opportunities.

West Germany and the Netherlands opposed the preferential regimes with associate countries due to the fear of the effects those new discriminatory trading systems could have on their trading partners in other parts of the world (Twitchett 1978:13–14; Mailafia 1997:44). Other specific reasons for their reluctance to include colonies came from their experiences in that period. The Netherlands was then coming out of the trauma of the Indonesian independence movement and did not want to be involved in any other new colonial engagements within the EEC; thus, the Dutch government did not even support the association status in the Treaty of Rome for its two remaining dependencies in the Netherlands Antilles and Surinam (Twitchett 1978:13; Mailafia 1997:44; Ravenhill 1985:50). The West German government opposed French demands, for fear of being engaged in supporting French colonialism through the EDF and thereby supporting France's repression of independence struggles in Algeria (Twitchett 1978:13–14).

France managed to persuade the other EEC partners to accept the association status for the colonies and a compromise was reached, whereby Germany agreed to contribute to the EDF but a special trading regime was extended to

German banana imports from Latin America (Article 15 of the Implementing Convention). To make sure that Germany also benefitted from preferential trade access, France had to accept a non-discriminatory right of establishment for companies from all six EEC member states in associated countries (Article 132, Paragraph 5 of Rome Treaty). Furthermore, the Dutch and the German governments were able to push for a five-year limit of association and managed to lower the EDF budget further than the French had requested (Ravenhill 1985:50).

The Treaty of Rome was signed in 1957 and Part IV, Articles 131–136 provided for the association status of overseas countries and territories. The treaty established a free trade area between the associates and the Community, thus exports from the associates (with the exception of certain sensitive products) would enter EEC countries duty-free without being subjected to the CET. Similarly, the associates were also required to abolish customs duties on imports from the Community and from each other according to the same timetable as that applicable to the six EEC members. However, associates could levy customs duties to facilitate their development and industrialisation procedures (Article 133). The Treaty of Rome also established the EDF to finance economic and social development in the associated territories. The first EDF had a budget of 581.25 million units of account (u/a) (at that time 1 u/a was equivalent to $1.00) and lasted for a five-year period, from 1958 to 1962 (Commission of the European Communities 1971). From then onwards, the fund continued to be provided to the associates and later to the ACP countries as a whole until 2020 during the 11th EDF. The EDF was financed through direct contributions from member states based on specific contribution keys and it was managed outside the framework of the EU general budget. EU member states maintained control of the EDF resources through the EDF committee, where they managed the fund in cooperation with the European Commission and the European Investment Bank (EIB). However, after the end of the 11th EDF in 2020, development programmes were supposed to be funded through the EU budget. The changes in receiving financial assistance via the EU budget also meant that the funding to ACP countries would be subjected "to the authorisation of the European Parliament and that the transactions have to comply with the EU financial regulations in the same way as other EU funded programmes" (European Commission 2022b:4).

In the early 1960s, when association status was in full swing, anti-colonial nationalist movements in African countries gathered momentum and soon the associated countries became independent. It was no longer possible to maintain the agreement which had been signed by the colonial powers on behalf of their colonies. Discussion emerged in the EEC about whether to continue with the associate status after the countries had achieved independence. Differences emerged again within the two camps: West Germany and the Netherlands on one side and France on the other. The former were hesitant about continuing to grant a special relationship exclusively towards Africa, whereas the latter preferred to renew extended association (Twitchett 1978:83; Migani 2013:19). In the end, it was decided to maintain the association agreement until its expiry in 1962.

During Yaoundé Conventions

The negotiations for the new agreement between the EEC and independent African countries started in mid-1961, culminating in the signing of the Yaoundé I Convention in 1963 between the six EEC member states and the 18 African countries which collectively became known as the Association of African and Malagasy States (AAMS).[2] The Convention extended the association regime for the next five years from 1964 to 1969. In the negotiations between the six EEC member states, France continued to defend its interests in Africa by advocating the continuation of a free trade zone and the continuation of sharing the costs of supporting its former colonies. France went further to propose aid that would compensate its former colonies for losses that would result from the abolition of the Franc Zone's guaranteed prices due to the existing European Common Market agreements. Germany and the Netherlands felt the preferential tariffs enjoyed by associated countries were a stumbling block for their other suppliers and wanted a larger framework to include non-associates (Zartman 1971:33). The other five, except for Belgium, were against the idea of providing aid to compensate the African countries coping with the end of guaranteed prices in the Franc Zone because they considered France to be shifting their own burdens onto the Community (Migani 2013:21–22). Italy, as shown in the previous section, supported the French position but was concerned with its own financial contribution, and was hesitant about this new additional aid for compensation. France managed to convince other EEC member states to continue to accept the free trade zone and to maintain association status; the rest maintained the possibility of trade with outside suppliers and gained an accelerated and reduced CET on tropical products with little compensation for the Africans (Zartman 1971:56–57). In this sense, the CET was reduced on certain tropical products, thus cutting the preferential tariff margin enjoyed by the associated states in relation to other countries (Twitchett 1978:85; Migani 2013:22). New aid for diversification and production was introduced to help the associated countries cope with the end of guaranteed prices in the Franc Zone. Germany and the Netherlands had to agree to the new aid for diversification, but they managed to shorten the period of disbursement (Twitchett 1978:86–87).

---

2 Burundi, Cameroon, Central African Republic, Chad, Congo-Brazzaville, Zaire (DR Congo), Dahomey (Benin), Gabon, Ivory Coast, Malagasy Republic (Madagascar), Mali, Mauritania, Niger, Rwanda, Senegal, Somalia, Togo and Upper Volta (Burkina Faso). Mauritius signed Yaoundé II in 1972, subsequently making the AAMS 19 countries.

The second Yaoundé Convention between the EEC and AAMS countries came into force in 1971 and extended cooperation until 1975. The negotiations for the agreement began in 1968 and coincided with discussions that took place during the second United Nations Conference on Trade and Development (UNCTAD) conference in New Delhi. The conference promoted the principle of the GSP for "developing countries" (Resolution 21 (ii) UNCTAD II Conference 1968). For that reason, during EEC internal negotiations regarding Yaoundé II, West Germany and the Netherlands considered changing the new system to benefit all "developing countries." West Germany and the Netherlands had important links with English-speaking African countries, Asia and Latin America (Migani 2013:27). France continued to favour the maintenance of free trade with the associated countries as well as the continual provision of aid for transformation and diversification (Twitchett 1978:117). By the end of the EEC internal negotiations, several concessions had been made. The trade regime continued to operate according to the free trade principle. However, the CET would be slightly reduced on certain tropical products of particular importance to Latin American and Asian countries. Aid for transformation and diversification, which was accepted reluctantly by Germany and the Netherlands in the Yaoundé I Convention, was eliminated in the new agreement; however, the associated countries were assured that in the event of a serious price collapse, aid for diversification could be provided (ibid.:117).

During the Yaoundé Conventions negotiations, the EEC opened up the policy to include some of the British former colonies, due to growing criticism of including only former French colonies. When Britain applied to join the EEC in 1961, it announced that its colonies would also get association status. This was highly criticised by African leaders of independent Commonwealth countries, who rejected Britain's initiatives to secure association without their consultation (Twitchett 1978:148; Mailafia 1997:51). Britain was denied membership in the Community due to the French veto, but the EEC opened the association status through a Declaration of Intent in 1963 to allow Commonwealth countries to apply for arrangements similar to those of the associates. Nigeria was the first to apply for trade preferences in 1963, followed by the EAC in 1969.[3] The Nigerian agreement did not enter into force, but the EAC's agreement was implemented simultaneously alongside other associate countries during the Yaoundé II Convention. The EEC's decision to open negotiations with the Commonwealth countries was not well received by the French, whereas other countries such as West Germany and the Netherlands welcomed the move because they wanted the EEC development goals to include the rest of Africa (Mailafia 1997:53; Migani 2013:25). The Nigerian decision to apply for trade preferences threatened French

---

3 This was during the first EAC, which was established in 1966 and collapsed in 1977.

interests in its former colonies. The French feared that Nigeria would later become the leader of the associates, so it tried to reduce the scope of the agreement (Migani 2013:25). In the end, the Lagos Agreement signed between Nigeria and the Community did not enter into force because of differences between France and Nigeria at the time of the Biafran War (Mailafia 1997:53; Bailey 1983:162). On the other hand, the Arusha Agreement between the EAC and the EEC was signed in 1969. It provided for tariff preferences for some exports from the EAC countries, and the countries also removed restrictions for some EEC exports. The agreement was restricted to trade. It did not include the provision of development aid such as the other AAMS countries in the Yaoundé agreement had.

Generally, although France got most of all that it wanted during this first phase, its dominance ended with the expiration of the Yaoundé II Convention. In the second phase, we will see how the admission of the UK to the EEC changed the dynamics of interstate bargaining and the geographical coverage of the EEC's development policy towards "developing countries." Furthermore, cooperation on the three instruments of aid, trade and, later, on political dialogue started to change to the favouring of a more globalist position.

During the Lomé Convention (1975–2000)

In 1973, Denmark, Ireland and the UK joined the Community, thus increasing the number of members from six to nine. The accession of the UK meant that association status would be changed to also include the British former colonies. Previously, Britain had twice applied to join the Community, in 1961 and 1967 respectively, but the French president Charles de Gaulle vetoed its entry due to, *inter alia*, the complications of integrating the British former colonies in the Yaoundé Conventions (Twitchett 1978:145–146; Mailafia 1997:63). After de Gaulle fell from power in 1969, Britain applied a third time in 1971 and was accepted. In the discussions around British accession to the Community and how to integrate its former colonies in the association agreement, France did not want the Commonwealth countries to interfere with the ongoing negotiation process. To this end, France proposed talks for a Yaoundé III Convention with the associates, where the Commonwealth countries would either have to join in or opt out (Mailafia 1997:63). On the other side, Germany and the Netherlands opposed the continuation of the French "regionalist" approach and preferred a globalist perspective for the Community's development policy towards a large group of "developing countries" (Ravenhill 1985:42; Mailafia 1997:63; Frisch 2013:111). After contentious internal discussions within the EEC, it was agreed to expand the Community's development focus towards Commonwealth countries in Africa, the Caribbean and the Pacific in the new agreement. The countries formed a united position as the ACP countries, consisting of 46 member states, a group which was established through the Georgetown Agreement of 1975. From then onwards, the ACP countries as a bloc became a strong focus of European development policy. Currently the ACP has 79 member states: 48 from sub-Saharan Africa, 16 from the Caribbean and 15 from the Pacific. The group was later reformed after adopting the revised Georgetown Agreement in 2020, which transformed the ACP group into the Organisation of African, Caribbean and Pacific States (OACPS). In reality, the accession of the UK meant the expansion of European policy from a focus on Africa alone to include British former colonies in the Caribbean and Pacific regions. As the globalist position improved due to the UK's accession, France had to compromise further, even when its position could not be adopted at the regional level. This second phase, constituting four Lomé Conventions signed after every five years, would confirm the assumption that powerful states are likely to make compromises and concessions when they are highly interested in adopting a certain agreement at regional level.

The Lomé I Convention between 46 ACP countries and nine EEC countries was signed in 1975, came into force in 1976 and covered the period until 1980. It led to substantial changes, especially on trade cooperation, and was widely referred to as a revolutionary agreement and a model which other "developed countries" should follow in their relations with "developing countries" (European Commission 1975). Major shifts during the Lomé Conventions were on trade arrangements from reciprocal to non-reciprocal trade preferences, which meant that the ACP countries' exports had free access to the EEC markets, and they were not obliged to open their markets for EEC goods as they had been under the Yaoundé Conventions. The negotiations within the EEC member states on changing to a non-reciprocal trade agreement were also divided along the two camps. The UK, on the one hand, supported by Ireland, the Netherlands and later by Germany, preferred changes towards non-reciprocal trade, whereas France, on the other hand, followed by Belgium, Italy and Luxembourg, demanded reciprocal trade regimes (Drieghe and Orbie 2009: 176–177). Later, however, it was the regionalist camp that gave in (ibid.). The pressure towards a non-reciprocal trade agreement came not only from intergovernmental bargaining but also from outside Europe. Some scholars point to the role of the new ACP Commonwealth countries with strong bargaining strategies, such as Jamaica, Guyana and Nigeria (Hewitt 1991:89). Also, global changes during the 1970s, such as the influence of the "Third World Countries" in pushing for the New International Economic Order in the United Nations systems that occurred with the oil price increases of 1973, together with the commodity boom, all strengthened the bargaining position of the ACP countries during the Lomé I Convention (Mailafia 1997:62–63; Bailey 1983:176–177; Ravenhill 1985: 14–22). Trade relationships between the EEC and ACP countries remained non-reciprocal for the whole period of the Lomé Conventions. Furthermore, ACP countries continued to receive aid through the EDF. In addition to the EDF, the Lomé

I Convention also established a system to subsidise ACP exports to the EEC known as Stabilization Export Earnings (Stabex). According to Ravenhill (1985:41), the new Stabex system could not only support the ACP exports but also ensured the future supply of raw materials in Europe.

The Lomé II Convention was signed in 1979 and was supposed to run until 1985. It preserved many of the features from the former convention. It introduced a system known as Sysmin to stabilise mineral exports from the ACP countries, which has been regarded as a strategic move by European countries to ensure sufficient supply of minerals to their countries (Clapham 1996:101). It was during the Lomé II Convention that the UK started pushing for the human rights conditionality that would become an important part of the political dialogue instrument with regard to the ACP countries. During the negotiations of the Lomé II Convention, the new conservative government in the UK, led by Margaret Thatcher, from 1979 to 1990 proposed to tie the benefits of the agreement with the condition that the ACP countries must respect human rights, as in the policies of the Structural Adjustment Programmes promoted by World Bank (WB) and International Monetary Fund (IMF) (Wall 1983:189–190; Hewitt 1991:90). Wall (1983:190) argued that the UK's proposition to include human rights conditionality targeted the then president of Uganda, Idi Amin. Furthermore, the UK was also interested in improving the effectiveness of the EDF and suggested that its allocations focus less on projects and instead adopt a World Bank style of economic programmes (Cumming 2013:69–70). This meant that the Community had to shift from the system of financing projects developed by ACP countries and, rather, follow certain policy programmes in order to ensure effectiveness. The French perceived the UK's proposal to change the European aid policies based on the WB and IMF as "part of an Anglo-Saxon conspiracy to undermine their position in ... francophone Africa" (Hewitt 1991:90). Despite the support the UK got from the Dutch government (Cumming 2013:69), the Lomé II Convention did not include the UK's demands. These propositions were also rejected by the ACP countries as well as some EEC member states (Hewitt 1991:91).

The Lomé III Convention was signed in 1984 and extended cooperation until 1990. Negotiations for it started in the early years during the Lomé II Convention. The UK's propositions on tying aid to human rights conditionality got support from the European Parliament, starting in 1983 (Cumming 2013:69). Furthermore, the European Commission also advocated the UK's position and proposed it to the member states. During Lomé III negotiations, Edgard Pisani, the then Development Commissioner, suggested changes towards policy dialogue in the programming phase of his 1982 memorandum (European Commission 1982). The Commission's proposition of policy dialogue was a way of changing the Community's development policy from a project-based approach towards the programming-oriented approach of Bretton Woods institutions as advanced by the UK during Lomé II negotiations (Cumming 2013:70). This change towards policy dialogue was included in the Lomé III Convention negotiations. This meant that exchange of views between the ACP and EEC countries would take place during the programming of aid resources culminating in a five-year indicative programme, and there would be a shift from projects financing – the construction of a road, for instance – towards sectoral supports – such as transport policy (Frisch 2008:18). The inclusion of policy dialogue in the Lomé III Convention was seen by the ACP countries as the new beginning of conditionality in the European aid system (Parfitt and Bullock 1990:107; Frisch 2008:18), a proposition which the ACP countries had rejected during the former Lomé II negotiation. However, in the mid-1980s, most of the ACP countries were experiencing economic decline and regions such as the Sahel and Southern Africa were hit by famine and droughts (Mailafia 1997:88–89); thus their bargaining power had also been weakened. The policy dialogue proposition, which also involved discussions related to the respect of human rights, was incorporated in the Lomé III Convention with major support from the Commission.

Lomé IV was the first Convention to cover a ten-year period (1990 to 2000), although a mid-term review of the Convention was scheduled for 1995. During the first Lomé IV negotiations, all the EEC member states fully agreed with the UK's proposition to follow WB structural adjustment programmes not only on human rights conditionality, which was accepted in the Lomé III Convention, but also on new conditionality in other aspects of democracy and economic reforms (European Council 1991). The negotiations to accept conditionalities in all these areas were again divided along the two major camps. The UK was also supported by the Netherlands and Germany, while France, Italy, Ireland and Belgium did not want the EEC aid to be linked to IMF and WB conditionalities (Mailafia 1997:98). Hewitt (1991:92) argues that it was in this period that EEC aid policy started moving to the position advanced by the British. Part of the EDF was used to support WB structural adjustment reforms (Hurt 2003:163; Mailafia 1997:110; Parfitt and Bullock 1990:108).

During the mid-term review of Lomé IV in 1995, there were various changes within and outside the EU which called for substantial reform for future agreements with the ACP countries. Changes at the EU level included the enlargement of the Community, which by 1995 consisted of 15 member states. Some new member states such as Greece, Portugal and Spain also needed financial support from the EU; therefore, the monetary aid budget also increased. This led to difficulties among the EU member states on the financial package of the EDF. Countries such as the UK, Germany, Italy and the Netherlands were reluctant to increase their contributions, but they later agreed on a minimum figure (Arts and Byron 1997:82–83). Some member states, especially the UK backed by the Netherlands, Italy and Germany, wanted the Community to pursue trade relationships with the ACP countries rather than providing aid (Cumming 2013:73). The end of the Cold War also led to a shift of interests within the EU, and some member states preferred to support the former communist countries within Europe rather than the ACP countries (Hugon 2013:97). These shifts within the EU meant that there was a need for changes in future EU–ACP agreements. Other impetuses for change came from beyond the EU, especially from the international trade community which regarded the trade relationship between the EU and the ACP countries under the Lomé Convention to be against international trade rules on non-discrimination. After the revision of the Lomé IV Convention in 1995, it became clear that reforms of the agreement between the EU and the ACP were necessary.

During the Cotonou Agreement (2000–2020)

The third phase of the Cotonou Agreement began in 2000 and was expected to end in 2020. During the negotiations towards the Cotonou Agreement, the difference among powerful states continued to exist, especially on the issues of trade and how to manage aid. The debate leading to changes towards the Cotonou Agreement was launched by the Commission's publication of a "Green Paper on Relations between the EU and the ACP Countries" in 1996 which proposed various options to reform EU–ACP relations (European Commission 1996). The green paper instigated extensive debate within EU countries, especially on the different options suggested for the geographical scope of the new agreement and its trade arrangements. On the geographical scope, the Commission proposed four major options: (i) to maintain the status quo by focusing on the ACP countries, but with some changes; (ii) to pursue a global overall agreement to be supplemented by bilateral agreements on a country-by-country basis or by groups of countries; (iii) to break up Lomé IV into regional agreements in sub-Saharan African, Caribbean and Pacific countries; and (iv) to establish a general agreement for the LDCs which could be opened up for non-ACP LDCs (ibid.:46–47). The EU member states were divided on this issue of EU–ACP relations. For instance, France and the UK wanted to continue the special relationship with the ACP group of countries (Forwood 2001:428–429; Carbone 2007:173; Posthumus 1998:9). Germany, on the other hand, wanted to "normalise" the EU–ACP relationship and suggested splitting the ACP group into three regional arrangements of African, Caribbean and Pacific countries (Forwood 2001:428; Carbone 2007:173). Denmark, Sweden, Finland and the Netherlands proposed equal treatment of all LDCs and suggested including another nine non-ACP LDCs into the ACP (Forwood 2001:428; Carbone 2007:173; Posthumus 1998:9).

The Commission also proposed four possible trade arrangements between the EU and ACP countries: (i) to maintain the status quo by preserving the non-reciprocal preferences to the ACP countries, but supplementing that with cooperation activities in trade-related fields; (ii) integration of the ACP countries into the EU's GSP, thus the LDC-ACP countries would be grouped with non-ACP LDCs, while the more advanced ACP countries would be included in the normal scheme; (iii) introduction of uniform reciprocity, whereby the ACP countries would introduce reciprocity after a transitional period; and (iv) introduction of differentiated reciprocity with different regional groups of ACP countries or between the EU and individual ACP countries (European Commission 1996:68–69). The EU member states, however, remained divided on trade. For example, France favoured the idea of free trade arrangements between the EU and the ACP regional groups, while the UK preferred the proposal of integrating the ACP countries into the EU's GSP (Posthumus 1998:5).

Other controversial issues in the negotiations towards the Cotonou Agreement were on aid allocation and the elements of political dialogue. On aid allocation, Germany and France had opposite positions, with the former preferring project aid and sectoral support, but the latter wanting the EU to stop project aid and move on towards direct budget support in combination with sectoral support; the UK wanted a flexible approach whereby a large bulk of resources would be allocated to the poorer countries, with a smaller part to be programmed (ibid.:10). On political dialogue, Germany and Italy were more concerned with the inclusion of migration during the political dialogue with the ACP countries (Posthumus 1998:3; Carbone 2007:174).

In the end, after several reactions from EU member states to the Commission's green paper, the member states had to come up with a common EU position so that the negotiations with the ACP countries could start. The Commission presented a negotiation directive for the new agreement, which the EU member states had to discuss in the Council. The negotiations in the Council lasted from January until May 1998. Within the Council, the controversial debates revolved around the two major objectives of trade liberalisation and regional integration. Liberalisation of the EU's agriculture markets, and the reduction of non-tariff barriers, were perceived as the best ways to improve ACP economies in the new agreement. On improving regional integration within the ACP countries, the establishment of Regional Economic Partnership Agreements (REPAs) were considered the most feasible option. Countries such as France, Italy, Spain and Portugal opposed the liberalisation of the EU's agriculture markets in order to protect their agricultural products, but they supported REPAs and saw them as a better solution for the ACP economies (Carbone 2007:173). The UK, the Netherlands and the Nordic countries were against REPAs and thought the approach would further marginalise the LDCs (Carbone 2007:173; Forwood 2001:428). In the end, the common EU position on the new agreement was passed: REPAs would be pursued in accordance with the World Trade Organisation waiver and access to EU markets for "essentially all products" coming from LDCs would be maintained (Forwood 2001:427–428).

After the EU countries had reached this common position, the negotiations with the ACP countries started in September 1998. First, however, the ACP countries also reacted to the Commission's proposal, especially on the trade arrangements, and called on the EU to maintain non-reciprocal trade preference and market access in the Libreville Declaration of 1997 (Declaration 30 of Libreville Declaration). During the negotiations, the ACP countries could not push through their preference on trade arrangements. They agreed to REPAs but managed to extend the transitional period (Forwood 2001:435). Another controversial topic during the negotiations was the definition of good governance included under political dialogue, which the ACP countries managed to change in scope (Commonwealth Secretariat 2004:197). The negotiations between the EU and the ACP countries culminated in the signing of the Cotonou Agreement in 2000 to last a period of 20 years. The Agreement entered into force in 2003 and made some changes in three areas of cooperation: trade arrangements, development assistance and political dialogue. Trade arrangements were to be changed towards reciprocal preferences based on free trade agreements to be concluded with ACP regions by December 2007. The allocation of development assistance would be based on ACP countries' performance. Some elements of providing aid based on performance had already started during the Lomé IV Convention. In the Cotonou Agreement, political dialogue included new issues such as peacebuilding, conflict prevention and resolution, migration and good governance. The Cotonou Agreement was reviewed twice. The first revision was signed in Luxembourg in 2005 and the second in Ouagadougou in 2010. New issues were incorporated in the revised Cotonou Agreement, such as security, and climate change and global warming.

During the third phase of the Cotonou Agreement, powerful states had different positions on various instruments of supporting regional integration; however, not all states managed to get their all positions adopted. Rather, each powerful state could only manage to achieve a certain position in at least one instrument, but not across all the policy items. France, which had to make so many concessions during the Lomé Convention period, was able to achieve its preference on trade. The three powerful countries had different preferences on how to address aid, but the UK's position was ultimately adopted. On political dialogue, Germany's position of including migration in the dialogue was accepted. This confirms further the assumption that each powerful state had to make concessions and compromises to ensure that they got something, and also had to give up some preferences. The situation in the third phase towards the Cotonou Agreement can be regarded as lowest-common-denominator bargaining among the powerful member states.

Current Post-Cotonou Agreement Negotiations

The Cotonou Agreement was supposed to end in 2020 and from 2021 it was supposed to be replaced by a new pact that would guide the relationship between EU and ACP countries in areas of aid, trade and political dialogue.

The negotiations for the new pact were concluded and the post-Cotonou Agreement was initialled on 15 April 2021. However, at the time of writing it has not been approved and ratified by ACP countries. The Cotonou Agreement, which was supposed to end in 2020, has been prolonged until the new pact enters into force once it has been ratified by all parties. Although current internal negotiations are not publicly available, the initialled text shows that all instruments to support regional integration (aid, trade and political dialogue) will continue to operate in almost the same ways as during the Cotonou Agreement.

Provision of aid to the ACP countries is expected to continue within the post-Cotonou Agreement if the initialled text enters into force. The only changes in terms of the aid that started in 2021 is the fact that the funds are no longer coming from the EDF but through the EU budget. In the current negotiated post-Cotonou Agreement text initialled by the EU and ACP countries in 2021, aid continues to be described as an important instrument of promoting regional integration. In Article 82, under Section 3 of the current negotiated agreement text, the EU outlines its commitment to use financial resources in facilitating regional, inter-regional and intercontinental cooperation and initiatives in ACP countries.

The trade policy of EPAs is also expected to continue in the post-Cotonou Agreement despite criticism and various challenges that have been directed towards the policy. Article 50 of the initialled text shows how EPAs continue to be a relevant instrument of trade cooperation. The article goes further in Section 7 to emphasise how EPAs are expected to intensify regional integration efforts and processes in ACP countries and to further encourage intra-ACP regional trade. The text also takes new developments in African countries into consideration, for instance, the launch of the African Continental Free Trade Area (AfCFTA) in 2021. Article 16 of the Africa regional protocol attached to the text shows that implementation of AfCFTA will be supported by both parties and EPAs are expected to contribute further to the deepening of continental trade in Africa.

Political dialogue as an important area of cooperation between EU and ACP countries has also been included in the current negotiated post-Cotonou Agreement. In addition to topics of dialogue discussed in Chapter 2, more themes have been added to the initialled pact. This has occurred mainly in the area of migration and mobility, which is one of the EU's major concerns towards African countries. Article 74 of the text calls all members of the OACPS to accept the return and readmission of their citizens who are illegally present in EU countries. Furthermore, the Africa regional protocol attached to the text shows, in Article 74, the importance of the EU and African countries working together in establishing legal migration pathways with a view to facilitating circular migration and mobility. All these are new critical issues that will have to be discussed through political dialogue and it remains to be seen if African countries will accept them.

The current phase of post-Cotonou Agreement negotiation shows almost a continuation of a similar position that was adopted during the previous Cotonou Agreement. This development confirms the assumption of path dependence in the outcome stage as suggested in the modified intergovernmentalism theoretical framework. Though internal negotiations towards the negotiated text are not yet publicly available, the continuation of a similar position shows how difficult it can be to change the various decisions adopted in the past. This can therefore explain why states would continue to accept the common EU development policy that allows for multilateral promotion of regional integration, despite their interests in using other bilateral channels. It is through the EU that states can also pursue collective European interests towards ACP regions, even though they might not have preferred a certain position during interstate bargaining. Such interests, as shown in previous chapters, involve economic and security goals as well as promotion of various norms. In the case of the EAC, as shown in Chapter 2, economic collective interests are pursued through encouraging partner states to sign the regional EPA that would require the bloc to open their markets gradually for EU products by 82.6% in 25 years. Security interests and promotion of norms, on the other hand, have been shown to be best pursued through political dialogue, whereby the EAC is supported in its various initiatives to promote peace in the region as well as good governance in its partner states. In addition to those collective interests, states might also have other specific national preferences towards different regional organisations, and thus they might decide to engage with those institutions through other bilateral channels. As we will see in the following second part of the book, those states with extra interests with regard to the EAC decided to utilise other bilateral means in their engagement with the bloc.

Part II
Bilateral Promotion of Regional Integration

4 National Interests and Regionalism Support

When states delegated power to the EU to run a common European development policy, they left room for themselves to pursue their own bilateral aid programmes. This enables them to pursue their own individual national interests towards specific countries and regions through their development policies. In this sense, states can use their foreign aid to prioritise other goals involving aid recipients. The three main bilateral strategies chosen by states to promote regional integration in the EAC, including the use of bilateral institutions, a non-profit company and the Partnership Fund, provide different opportunities for donor countries to pursue their different national interests in the region. In each of these bilateral strategies, development partners can engage with the EAC in various formats based on what they want to achieve in the region.

Use of bilateral institutions to promote regional integration, for instance, provides flexibility for donor countries in their support of the EAC via their national development agencies. Donors can start their own regional policy programmes towards the region and implement them via their own institutions. As shown in Table 1.1 in the introductory chapter, this has been a strategy mainly employed by Germany in its support of the EAC. The country uses its own national development agency, the *Deutsche Gesellschaft für Internationale Zusammenarbeit* (GIZ), and has established various policy programmes to finance integration activities in different sectors. Through using its own national development agencies, Germany can flexibly support what it wants to in the region, based on its own national preferences towards the EAC. Furthermore, the strategy provides independence for Germany to engage with the EAC in a unique way. However, for a donor country to be able to use this strategy, it needs to have high capacity, not only in terms of finances to start its own regional policy programmes, but also in ensuring that its national development agencies are able to operate at the regional level.

Use of a non-profit company, TMEA, is another bilateral strategy that is preferred by some EU member states to promote regional integration in the EAC. Through this strategy, donors provide finance to support regionalism activities to TMEA, and the company oversees implementation of the projects on their behalf. In this way, those donors who do not wish to implement their

DOI: 10.4324/9781003290155-6

own regional policy programmes towards the EAC via their national development agencies are able to delegate their activities to TMEA. As such, states with high capacity to use their bilateral institutions can also decide to use TMEA strategically in implementing their integration initiatives in the region. On the other hand, use of a non-profit company could also offer a possibility for small donors interested in the EAC, but without huge capacity, to simply contribute to TMEA's integration activities.

Use of the Partnership Fund is also an important bilateral channel employed by most donor countries in their support of the EAC. Through this channel, donors mainly contribute their finances in a basket fund so that the money can be used by the EAC to finance their different integration activities and programmes. The fund offers an opportunity for all donors interested in supporting the EAC to offer financial contributions without earmarking them to specific projects of interest. Furthermore, by contributing to the fund, donors do not have to establish their own regional policy programmes and implement them via their institutions or through TMEA, because the EAC itself oversees them. In this sense, the fund can also be an effective strategy for small donors with less capacity, but with interests in the region, to engage in supporting the EAC through contributions. Once they have contributed financially to the Partnership Fund, they do not have to do anything else and are still regarded as promoters of regional integration.

All these three bilateral channels provide different opportunities for donor countries to engage with the EAC. As shown in Table 1.1, donors can also use more than one channel. Germany, for instance, employs its bilateral institutions, but also contributes to the Partnership Fund. Furthermore, most of the countries using TMEA to support integration also contribute to the Partnership Fund. The question is therefore raised, in this second part of the book, as to why countries decide to choose bilateral strategies if they are able to support integration at the multilateral level via the EU. In addition, why do states also choose different bilateral strategies in their support of regional integration in the EAC? Foreign policy analysis approaches can provide explanations on why states would make certain decisions. In this chapter, we will explore the three main foreign policy analysis approaches based on power, interests and norms/identity, to explain EU member states' choices in their bilateral promotion of regional integration.

Power-Based Approach

The power-based approach stems from an international relations theory of neorealism, which regards states' interests to be determined by the distribution of power in the international system (Waltz 1979). This is due to the anarchic structure of the international system that raises the problem of security, and as such, powerful states will do whatever they can to maintain their position of power in order to ensure their own survival (ibid.:105). In this sense, even when states join or create a transnational institution such as the EU, their aim is to use such organisations to pursue their own interests (Mearsheimer 1994; Hyde-Price 2006). Strong states will always seek to operate autonomously and influentially even when they interact with other countries within international institutions. That is also the case when a common policy exists to support regional integration at the multilateral level; powerful states want to act independently outside the EU context and employ their own bilateral strategies.

Development aid policy can be considered a foreign policy tool by donor countries to pursue their strategic interests in recipient countries and regions. Obviously, the EAC countries do not pose serious security threats to Europe, for instance through increasing their relative power position or improving their offensive capabilities, as neorealists would argue (Waltz 1979; Mearsheimer 1994); however, as shown in previous chapters, instability in African countries is regarded as having negative impacts on EU security, for instance through illegal migration and refugee flows. Supporting African regional integration processes through the EU and bilateral channels can also be a means of dealing with those perceived security challenges. As regional organisations bring together groups of countries, states might strategically use them in promoting security within a specific region. In this way, development aid can be used to establish policy programmes to support peace and security within the framework of a regional organisation. On the other hand, donors can also promote peace indirectly by supporting economic growth. Initiatives to support regional economic integration, for instance, can also be considered by donors as a means of driving economic growth in a specific region, thus leading to peace. This is due to the assumption that growth will generate high income and convince people to approve of their governments, thereby generating stability (Kant 2006). Such arguments linking economic growth to peace and political stability, however, do not stem from a neorealist point of view, but rather from a liberal perspective.

Although powerful states are expected to act autonomously, given their relative power position as compared to other countries, neorealists also consider other factors such as historical links in determining states' foreign policy decisions (Walt 1995:223–226). In the previous chapter, we have seen how colonial ties can influence the positions of powerful EU states when coordinating different phases of the EU's development policy towards the EAC and the ACP countries in general. Colonial ties between powerful EU countries and the EAC's partner states, can also influence how donors choose their bilateral channels to support integration. It can therefore be expected that powerful EU member states with colonial ties to EAC countries are likely to either use bilateral institutions or autonomously use the non-profit company in their promotion of regional integration. This is due to the flexibility the two channels offer to donors in their pursuit of strategic interests. Through their own bilateral institutions, donors can start their regional policy programmes and implement them independently. This is also possible when they use TMEA, where they can design their regional policy programmes to be implemented by the company. On the other hand, as through the Partnership Fund in which donors simply contribute their finances to be used by the EAC, the strategy can be regarded as another possible avenue through which powerful EU member states can support the EAC in addition to other bilateral channels of their interest.

The power-based assumption would mainly explain the decisions by powerful EU member states, which are mainly France and Germany, but also the UK when it was still a member of the EU. The questions raised based on their engagement with the EAC include: why is Germany actively involved in the EAC with its bilateral institutions, but also contributing to the partnership fund? Why did other powerful states, France and the UK, decide to use the non-profit company in addition to contributing to the Partnership Fund? And why does Germany not use the non-profit company, whereas France and the UK do not use their bilateral institutions in their engagement with the EAC? In responding to these questions, we will explore states' foreign policy strategies towards regional organisations, their historical ties with EAC countries as well as their approaches in dealing with security challenges in African countries. All these factors proposed by the power-based approach may explain why powerful states chose certain bilateral strategies in their support of the EAC.

Interest-Based Approach

Other interests, apart from security concerns as suggested by neorealists, can also play a strong role in states' decisions to use bilateral channels. The international relations theory of neoliberal institutionalism considers economic interests to be an important factor in understanding states' behaviour. For example, when there are high levels of economic interdependence among countries, states are more likely to adopt policies which enable them to preserve those economic ties (Keohane and Nye 1977). As such, economic interests may facilitate states in pursuing cooperative policies in order to maintain financial benefit (Powell 1993:211). This is due to complex interdependencies that can occur at the international level, whereby states are bonded together in patterns of mutual dependence (Burton 1972). As a result, states care more about their individual absolute gains, specifically how they will benefit from cooperating with others (Powell 1993:209).

Foreign development aid could be an example of an instrument pursued by states to maintain their economic benefits towards recipient countries and regions. This can explain why EU member states delegated power to the EU to run a common European development policy, but they also left room for their bilateral development programmes. As shown in the previous chapters, trade conditionality was used within the EU's development policy to pursue common European economic interests. The EPA's trade policy, for instance, has been used by the EU to enter free trade agreements with different regional blocs of ACP countries. In this sense, the EU might create opportunities for member states, but it is the task of individual countries to ensure they reap those benefits, and this can be facilitated by their bilateral development programmes. In this regard, even when it comes to the promotion of regional integration, states choose their bilateral strategies based on the economic benefits they gain from a specific region. Furthermore, regional integration processes can also lead to formation of large markets among neighbouring countries, thus offering potential future economic benefits for donor countries in terms of their trade and investments.

According to neoliberal institutionalists, states pursue friendly foreign policies towards other nations and regions that offer them economic gains. Given this line of thought, when it comes to selection of bilateral strategies to promote regional integration in the EAC, it can therefore be expected that those countries with the most economic benefit from the region are more likely to actively support integration via their bilateral institutions or through active use of the non-profit company. This is due to the potentials of these two channels in enabling donor countries to establish their own policy programmes that fit their economic interests towards the region. In the same vein, those countries which benefit economically from the EAC can additionally support the bloc through contributing to the Partnership Fund. The assumptions provided in this section would explain why EU member states chose bilateral institutions and TMEA in addition to the Partnership Fund. This is linked to states' economic benefits, by assessing their trade gains in the EAC countries in terms of exports and imports. Furthermore, states' foreign policy strategies towards Africa will be assessed to examine how they intend to pursue economic interests in other regions.

Norm/Identity-Based Approach

The norm/identity-based approach is associated with the constructivism theory of international relations, which emphasises the importance of other factors such as norms and identity in explaining states' foreign policy decisions. Constructivists reject the idea that states' foreign policy decisions are based on their power positions and interests, as argued by neorealists and neoliberal institutionalists respectively. Rather, they consider states' socially constructed ideas play a central role in understanding their foreign policy interests. Norms, in this regard, are defined as "intersubjectively shared, value-based expectations of appropriate behaviour" (Boekle et al. 2001:106). It is norms that determine state behaviour and, hence they "legitimize goals and thus define actors' interests" (Klotz 1995:26); furthermore, the norms states would adhere to in their interactions with other nations "constitute social identities and give national interests their content and meaning" (Adler 2013:126). In this sense, to understand why states chose specific bilateral strategies in their support of the EAC, it is necessary to understand their norms and identities as to what they regard as appropriate ways of pursuing their interests by promoting integration.

The EU, as explained in the introduction chapter, has always been associated with the identity as a promoter of integration within Europe and in other parts of the world. This norm can spread to its member states and can be the reason why some countries have adopted it in their own foreign development aid policy, thereby using other bilateral channels to promote integration in the EAC. In this sense, states may have internalised the norm of integration and consider the promotion of regionalism to be the best and most appropriate way of also pursuing their national interests in other regions. However, even though norm internalisation could have taken place, states might have established different unique identities in specific regions and that may also explain why they would prefer certain bilateral channels over others. In this context, it can be expected that states that consider promotion of regional integration as an appropriate way of pursuing their national interests and which also intend to preserve a distinct identity in the region, are more likely to use their bilateral institutions in supporting the EAC. On the other hand, states that do not intend to preserve a unique identity, but which still regard promotion of integration as an appropriate and effective way of pursuing their interests, would use the non-profit company or contribute to the Partnership Fund. As the use of the non-profit company and the Partnership Fund involves many donor countries, states cannot pursue their unique identities in the region as compared to if they were to employ their bilateral institutions. The role of norms and identities will be assessed through examining how officials, as well as foreign policies and strategies of those specific EU member states, regard promotion of integration.

Norms, according to constructivists, can also originate from international institutions and be shared globally by states (Finnemore 1996; Boekle et al. 2001). One such norm when it comes to development aid is the significance of donor coordination in improving aid effectiveness, which has been emphasised in different international forums in Rome, Paris, Accra and Busan in 2003, 2005, 2008 and 2011 respectively. Considering this, states are also expected to follow the norm of donor coordination in their selection of bilateral strategies. Comparing the bilateral channels of supporting integration in the EAC, donor coordination mainly occurs in the framework of the Partnership Fund, since all development partners put their finances to the EAC in a basket, and the bloc can use it to finance their integration activities more freely. Coordination might also occur within the non-profit company since different donors contribute to the activities of TMEA in the region; however, implementation and management of projects is not done by the EAC itself but rather by the company. In light of this, it can be expected that states are more likely to additionally use the Partnership Fund to show that they coordinate their aid at the recipient level. This assumption would explain why most of the EU member states chose to contribute to the fund in addition to other bilateral channels of their interests. However, Table 1.1 shows that Ireland and the Netherlands are the only countries which do not contribute to the Partnership Fund and rely solely on the non-profit company. The question that will also be analysed based on this decision is whether the two countries do not believe in donor coordination or if they have other reasons for sticking to the non-profit company only.

National Interests and Regionalism Analysis

This chapter has provided different potential explanations as to what motivates countries to support integration beyond the EU and why they choose different bilateral strategies to do so. States can use their aid to pursue their national preferences towards recipients. Regional organisations can provide an opportunity for donor countries to secure those interests even with a group of countries in a specific region. In other words, regional organisations can be regarded as new possibilities for states to pursue their interests beyond individual countries of their concern. The foreign policy analysis approaches adopted in this chapter provide assumptions on why states might choose specific bilateral strategies based on their national preferences in the EAC.

The theories provide different variables on where states' interests originate, in explaining their choices of bilateral strategies. As shown in this chapter, the three variables that have been selected to explain the outcome in the EAC involve power position, economic interests as well as norms/identity. As some of these selected factors follow different logics and ontological assumptions in explaining states choices, I will assess which theoretical approach better explains states' choices. In circumstances whereby more than one theory explains the outcome, I will provide an analysis of the conditions under which different theoretical assumptions can be linked to explain states' choices. Scholars call this challenge, of including more than one variable in explaining an outcome without ordering their importance, "explanatory over-determinacy" (Dür 2011:186). To avoid this problem, the following empirical chapter will also categorise those variables in terms of what might be considered causal factors and those that might have provided sufficient conditions leading to the outcome. Furthermore, in responding to different questions raised in this second part of the book, I rely mainly on states' foreign policy documents and their development policy strategies and programmes towards African countries and regions, as well as other secondary literatures that have dealt with similar topics. Interviews with officials working in those European programmes to support integration in the EAC are also used. Major questions that were asked of those officials include: why do European countries decide to support the EAC outside the EU multilateral channel?

The case of the EAC provides an opportunity to understand the specific interests of EU member states when they engage with regional organisations.

Assumptions proposed in this part of the book can also be used in other African regions and beyond, where similar circumstances of regionalism promotion occur. Powerful EU member states, and those with interests towards a certain regional organisation, are likely to adopt independent bilateral policies when engaging with regions that interest them. Their engagement with those regions, however, differ, based on states' capacities to execute those bilateral strategies. Some states with low capacity in the region might decide to mainly participate in collaborative programmes with other donors, whereas those with high capacity might want to introduce their own policy programmes implemented by their own bilateral institutions or a non-profit company. Let us now move on to the empirical chapter and explore why states chose specific bilateral strategies in their promotion of regional integration in the EAC.

5 How States Choose

How states choose their bilateral strategies when they promote regional integration outside the EU context depends on various factors. In the context of this book, variables determining states' choices are derived from foreign policy analysis approaches based on power, interests as well as norms/identity. These factors proposed by international relations theories of neorealism, neoliberal institutionalism and constructivism respectively, are expected to play a strong role in state's selection of bilateral strategies to support regionalism in the EAC, whether through their bilateral institutions, a non-profit company or the Partnership Fund. The general question asked in this chapter is, therefore, why EU member states choose specific bilateral strategies in addition to their multilateral support of regional integration. In addition to that general question, there are other unique choices made by states that will be analysed in this chapter (see again Table 1.1 on how states chose their bilateral strategies). Germany, for instance, is the only country that uses its own bilateral institutions. On the other hand, Ireland and the Netherlands rely only on the non-profit company and are the only countries which do not contribute to the Partnership Fund. Therefore, while examining selection of bilateral institutions, we will not only explore why Germany selected its own development agencies to support the EAC, but also why other countries did not follow that approach. Through using the non-profit company, on the other hand, we will assess why most of the countries, except Germany, rely on TMEA. Finally, we will also examine why most of the countries contribute to the Partnership Fund in addition to their other bilateral strategies, apart from the Netherlands and Ireland. Now let's dive into each of these bilateral strategies and explore how the selected variables of power, interests and norms/identity explain states' choices.

Use of Bilateral Institutions

Germany, as the only country that actively supports the EAC through its own bilateral institutions, follows a unique approach when it comes to foreign aid. The Federal Ministry for Economic Cooperation and Development is in charge of coordinating Germany's development cooperation. The ministry normally

DOI: 10.4324/9781003290155-7

implements its activities via different bilateral institutions based on whether it provides technical or financial assistance. The *Deutsche Gesellschaft für Internationale Zusammenarbeit* (GIZ) would typically implement technical assistance, whereas financial support is mainly executed by its government-owned development bank, the *Kreditanstalt für Wiederaufbau* (KfW). This is also the case in the EAC whereby Germany's support is implemented through technical and financial assistance via different agencies. In addition to the GIZ, part of technical assistance to the EAC is also implemented by Germany's national metrology institute, the *Physikalisch-Technische Bundesanstalt* (PTB).

In the provision of technical assistance through the GIZ and the PTB, the German government is able to flexibility and independently engage with the EAC through financing projects corresponding to its interests. Currently, the GIZ is focusing on three core projects in the areas of regional economic integration, digital innovation and health. The GIZ project to boost economic integration, which is also co-financed by the EU, is called "Support to East African Market-Driven and People-Centred Integration" and is currently in its second phase, from 2022 to 2025. During the first phase of the project from 2019 to 2022, a budget of EUR 13.4 million was allocated to finance its activities. Out of that amount, EUR 10.6 million came from the German government, whereas EUR 2.8 million came from the EU (GIZ 2021:6). A project on supporting regional digital innovation, known as "Digital Skills for an Innovative East African Industry," has been allotted EUR 5.7 million for its current phase from 2021 to 2024 (ibid.:9). In addition, the GIZ also established a project in the health sector called "Support to Pandemic Preparedness in the EAC Region" and its phase from 2019 to 2022 was earmarked a budget of EUR 4.7 million (ibid.:10). Furthermore, the PTB, has also been involved in the EAC since 2004 through implementing a programme known as the EAC-PTB programme "Establishment of a Regional Quality Infrastructure in the EAC," which is currently in its fifth phase from 2019 to 2023. The EAC-PTB programme aims to support improvements in EAC's products in terms of quality assurance and compliance with relevant standards as well as to enhance their safety for consumer consumption in both domestic and international markets (PTB 2022).

Germany's financial assistance, on the other hand, has been directly provided to the EAC through its government-owned bank, the KfW development bank. In this context, the EAC is now in charge of implementing different projects supported by Germany and not the GIZ and PTB, as in the area of technical assistance. One of the major financial contributions to the EAC included EUR 14 million that financed the construction of the EAC headquarters (BMZ 2011). According to a German diplomat "the construction of the EAC headquarters is Germany's most visible support to the EAC" (Interview with German diplomat, Dar es Salaam, 27 April 2015). Generally, the German government started to assist and consult the EAC in 1999 when the organisation was in the early stages of reviving its integration process (EAC Germany 2022a; Interview with Germany's GIZ official, Arusha, 7 May 2015). Since then, Germany has committed more than EUR 580 million for development cooperation with the EAC by providing financial and technical assistance in the region (EAC Germany 2022a). All of Germany's initiatives raise the question of why the country is actively involved in supporting the EAC and uses its bilateral institutions to do so. In the same vein, why are other countries not employing similar strategies? As argued in the previous chapter, the use of national bilateral institutions requires high capacities of those agencies in terms of finance and the ability to start their own policy programmes. Therefore, throughout this section I will compare Germany to other powerful states – France and the UK – while asking why the other two have not used their bilateral institutions despite their ability to do so. The three foreign policy approaches – power, interests and norms/identity – provide different explanations on this outcome.

Power-Based Approach

Germany's decision to use its bilateral institutions confirms the assumptions of neorealists that powerful countries aim to maintain their positions of power and seek independence in pursuing their security interests in other parts of the world. Germany's current policy guidelines for Africa regard the armed conflicts, wars and violence that take place in some African countries as also having a negative impact in Europe, for instance, through displacement and irregular migration, cross-border organised crime and terrorism (Federal Foreign Office 2019:7). In dealing with these perceived security challenges, Germany's policy guidelines for Africa identify its commitment to crisis prevention, stabilisation, conflict resolution and peacebuilding on the continent (ibid.). To that end, the policy regards the African Union (AU) and African regional organisations as important partners in conflict prevention and resolution (ibid.:8). The EAC is regarded by Germany as one of those African regional organisations that is essential in promoting peace and security on the continent. According to a German diplomat, the German government considers the EAC one of its major foreign policy partners in dealing with security problems in the region, and to signal this to the bloc, various high-level German officials, such as the president, have made an official visit to the EAC headquarters (Interview with German diplomat, Dar es Salaam, 27 April 2015).

Promoting peace and security is one of the areas in which Germany supported the EAC through a programme called the EAC-GIZ programme "Support to Peace and Security in the EAC," which operated from 2006 to 2014. The programme focused on controlling the proliferation of small arms and light weapons, strengthening the Peace and Security Department of the EAC Secretariat and enabling the involvement of non-state actors in peace and security processes in the region (GIZ 2016). Currently, Germany continues to support peace and security within the EAC through an associated project at the AU level, which is called African Union Border Programme (AUBP). The project intends to promote peace, security and stability through delimitation and demarcation of borders, cross-border cooperation and capacity building (African Union 2022). Within this programme, Germany introduced a project called the GIZ-AUBP in 2008 which targets different members of the AU, including the EAC as a bloc. In this context, the EAC has mainly been supported in mitigating cross-border security threats through, for instance, establishment of conflict early-warning mechanisms and facilitating engagement of local cross-border committees in prevention of disputes between border communities (EAC Germany 2022b).

Although Germany may have used its bilateral institutions for the purpose of seeking flexibility in pursuing its security concerns in the EAC, neorealists also consider the importance of historical ties in determining states' decisions towards specific regions. Germany has colonial ties with some countries in the EAC, although its colonisation ended after its defeat in the First World War in 1919. EAC member states including Burundi, Rwanda and the Tanzanian mainland were former German colonies, forming what was known as German East Africa. After losing the First World War, the first two countries were mandated to Belgium, and the latter to the UK. Thus, Germany's active engagement in the EAC through the use of its bilateral institutions could be seen as a way of reactivating strong partnership with a regional organisation that constitutes many of its former colonies concentrated in one regional bloc. Germany's other African former colonies of Namibia, Togo and Cameroon belong to different regional organisations in Southern Africa Development Community (SADC), Economic community of West African States (ECOWAS) and Economic Community of Central African States (ECCAS) respectively.

While all the arguments analysed here, based on security concerns as well as historical ties, can explain why Germany might have used its bilateral institutions to support the EAC, the question that remains is why other powerful countries (France and the UK) have not adopted a similar approach. To begin with the historical ties argument, France does not have colonial linkages with EAC countries, so that might be the reason it is not actively involved in the EAC. In West Africa, where it has colonial ties, for instance, France actively uses its bilateral institution known as the *Agence française de développement* (AFD) to support ECOWAS in its various integration projects (AFD 2015). On the other hand, though the UK has colonial ties with Kenya and Uganda in the EAC bloc, as we saw in Chapter 2, its other former colonies are spread throughout different parts of Africa, so using its bilateral institutions to support integration may not be enough to cover all the regions. In terms of pursuing security interests, the two countries have other instruments through which they can deal with perceived security threats from Africa. They are among the five permanent members of the United Nations Security Council, where most of the African peacekeeping mechanisms are decided. They can also promote peace and security in Africa through their post-colonial international organisations – the Commonwealth and Francophonie for the UK and France, respectively. In their security strategies, France and the UK emphasise the use of the Security Council as well as post-colonial international organisations to promote peace and security (HM Government 2015 and French White Paper on Defence and National Security 2013). Germany does not have such international organisations or a veto power in the Security Council to effectively promote peace and security in African countries, thus it is possibly relying on some regional organisations. The EAC as a regional organisation, with many of its former colonies, provides a great opportunity for Germany to actively support its integration while at the same time pursuing its security concerns.

Interest-Based Approach

Economic interests could have motivated Germany to actively engage with the EAC through its bilateral institutions. Based on neoliberal institutionalism, it has been assumed that states which benefit economically from the EAC would prefer to use their national bilateral institutions in their support of regionalism. Table 5.1 shows trade earnings between Germany and five older members of the EAC and Table 5.2 depicts its commercial relationship with Nigeria and South Africa. This data shows that Germany benefits more, commercially, in Africa through trading with Nigeria and South Africa than with the EAC countries. Although there is a significant increase of trade between Germany and Tanzania, Kenya and Uganda, the earnings are rather low compared to Nigeria and South Africa. In this sense, the interest-based approach through measuring trade earnings alone cannot explain its decision to use bilateral institutions, since EAC countries are not important trade partners to Germany. Commercial benefits can only be considered in terms of future economic gains that might result from successful integration in the EAC. However, that would mean moving from material factors proposed by neoliberal institutionalism to immaterial and ideational assumptions based on constructivism, proposing promotion of regional integration via bilateral institutions as the best way of achieving future economic gains. Such prospects can be seen in Germany's Africa Strategy of 2011, whereby the government regards the promotion of regional integration as its first priority towards economic development in Africa that would also create future opportunities for German businesses on the continent (Federal Foreign Office 2011:29–35). In Germany's most recent Africa strategy, the importance of Africa's economic development through foreign trade and investments is also emphasised, especially in benefitting individuals involved in business in Germany and Africa (Federal Foreign Office 2019:14). Earlier in this section, we saw how Germany's initiatives intend to facilitate regional economic integration,

Table 5.1 Germany's Exports and Imports to and from EAC Countries, 2010–2014 (in Million US Dollars)

	Exports					Imports				
	Tanzania	Kenya	Uganda	Rwanda	Burundi	Tanzania	Kenya	Uganda	Rwanda	Burundi
2010	165.04	320.32	144.01	32.62	6.44	94.42	91.48	97.50	14.40	2.31
2011	203.87	354.47	151.75	36.05	23.85	201.60	84.08	117.41	15.70	3.31
2012	245.58	484.16	132.87	47.67	15.20	159.07	113.88	96.00	9.92	7.00
2013	209.52	429.18	104.45	46.93	24.45	153.62	94.38	110.70	9.83	12.79
2014	249.91	531.29	138.63	41.80	20.67	189.13	121.08	110.10	26.20	5.62

Source: IMF Direction of Trade Statistics (DOTS)

Table 5.2 Germany's Exports and Imports to and from Sub-Saharan Africa, South Africa and Nigeria, 2010–2014 (in Million US Dollars)

	Exports			Imports		
	SSA	South Africa	Nigeria	SSA	South Africa	Nigeria
2010	14,879.65	10,108.97	1,412.37	11,614.88	6,104.24	2,533.41
2011	17,899.01	12,011.85	1,773.48	16,857.93	7,172.75	4,793.47
2012	17,118.62	11,307.94	1,615.20	14,489.19	5,233.74	5,670.89
2013	17,428.28	11,313.11	1,763.16	14,144.44	5,017.89	5,431.26
2014	17,522.42	11,015.95	1,823.79	13,210.67	5,230.24	5,251.84

Source: IMF Direction of Trade Statistics (DOTS)

for instance, through its current GIZ project "Support to East African Market-Driven and People-Centred Integration." The success of such projects could facilitate economic development in the EAC and offer future economic benefits to German companies in accessing a large regional market for their products and investments.

While Germany does not earn much from trading with EAC countries and its use of bilateral institutions seems to be explained by ideational factors, including the expectation of future commercial gains, what about the other powerful countries? Why are they not using their bilateral institutions despite their ability to do so? Comparing the trade relations of France and the UK with the five EAC countries as well as with Nigeria and South Africa, similar trends are observed (see Tables 5.3 and 5.4 for France and Tables 5.5 and 5.6 for the UK). As in the case of Germany, both France and the UK earn more from trading with Nigeria and South Africa than with EAC countries. The two countries also anticipate future economic benefits from African countries, but they use other strategies to pursue them. The UK, for instance, connects its aid to the general global prosperity goal, which provides opportunities for the UK's trade and investment but does not clearly connect that to the promotion of regional integration (HM Treasury 2015). France is also interested in the economic opportunities in African countries and regards the deepening of regional integration as the best way to pursue that; however, its development cooperation vision emphasises the pursuit of those interests through supporting development mainly at the national level (Ministry of Foreign and European Affairs 2011:38–39). France considers that its development support in the individual EAC countries also scales up integration in the region more broadly, and so does not see the need to establish its own policy programme to support integration in the EAC through its bilateral institutions (Interview with French diplomat, Dar es Salaam, 9 June 2015). Neither France nor the UK connects their aid policies to the promotion of regional integration as a means of pursuing their economic interests, as Germany does; this may explain why fostering regional integration through their bilateral institutions is not a major priority for them. In this sense, the two countries are comfortable with using TMEA and pursue their future economic gains via the company. Furthermore, as implied earlier, the two countries can also pursue their economic interests directly through their post-colonial international organisations and do not have to rely much on regional organisations.

Norm/Identity-Based Approach

Ideational and immaterial goals such as norms and identity have been proposed by constructivists to explain states' decisions. In this regard, Germany is assumed to have internalised the norm of integration and to consider regionalism promotion as an appropriate way of pursuing national interests and preserving its unique identity towards the EAC. Germany's positive

Table 5.3 French Exports and Imports to and from EAC Countries, 2010–2014 (in Million US Dollars)

	Exports					Imports				
	Tanzania	Kenya	Uganda	Rwanda	Burundi	Tanzania	Kenya	Uganda	Rwanda	Burundi
2010	196.99	226.55	89.77	16.09	24.33	18.65	62.88	13.77	2.78	0.50
2011	108.51	220.90	100.86	22.72	32.22	27.77	64.05	16.80	4.70	1.45
2012	185.34	315.96	100.67	22.81	25.45	28.99	58.49	14.21	4.04	0.40
2013	41.00	237.37	126.71	20.45	20.32	123.08	62.97	20.95	3.59	4.97
2014	68.89	252.58	95.69	24.83	21.25	39.43	65.32	20.66	2.96	4.81

Source: IMF Direction of Trade Statistics (DOTS)

Table 5.4 French Exports and Imports to and from Sub-Saharan Africa, South Africa and Nigeria, 2010–2014 (in Million US Dollars)

	Exports			Imports		
	SSA	South Africa	Nigeria	SSA	South Africa	Nigeria
2010	14,409.03	2,397.14	2,096.96	11,043.04	1,043.31	3,365.49
2011	16,980.76	3,312.49	2,068.54	15,445.20	1,022.29	5,991.96
2012	15,030.30	2,508.34	1,742.43	14,926.09	816.78	4,761.21
2013	15,630.98	2,496.17	2,034.80	14,410.18	811.75	5,024.69
2014	16,012.73	2,675.71	2,019.53	14,138.50	822.63	5,497.11

Source: IMF Direction of Trade Statistics (DOTS)

Table 5.5 The UK's Exports and Imports to and from EAC countries, 2010–2014 (in Million US Dollars)

	Exports					Imports				
	Tanzania	Kenya	Uganda	Rwanda	Burundi	Tanzania	Kenya	Uganda	Rwanda	Burundi
2010	180.78	391.90	87.45	-	-	34.56	519.88	17.67	7.32	-
2011	348.50	558.33	100.12	-	-	39.72	587.54	22.42	-	-
2012	279.19	598.77	99.79	20.68	-	39.00	499.41	23.09	-	-
2013	262.78	659.79	75.44	-	-	37.58	470.77	26.91	-	-
2014	268.17	629.91	73.88	-	-	56.71	422.23	25.53	5.65	-

Source: IMF Direction of Trade Statistics (DOTS)

Table 5.6 The UK's Exports and Imports to and from Sub-Saharan Africa, South Africa and Nigeria, 2010–2014 (in Million US Dollars)

	Exports			Imports		
	SSA	South Africa	Nigeria	SSA	South Africa	Nigeria
2010	10.959.83	3.924.93	2.015.08	14.180.23	9.200.80	1.233.85
2011	14.633.70	5.817.31	2.371.21	21.474.58	9.823.82	3.623.62
2012	13.638.80	3.912.05	2.128.94	24.071.89	9.673.58	6.006.71
2013	12.009.94	3.835.10	2.135.74	18.820.24	4.426.49	4.828.27
2014	10.918.74	3.740.83	2.136.34	16.915.31	7.475.25	4.049.51

Source: IMF Direction of Trade Statistics (DOTS)

integration experiences within the EU are said to have motivated the country to internalise the norm of integration and promote regionalism in other parts of the world. These experiences, according to a GIZ official, include its economic growth resulting from the wider European market and solving its old historical conflicts especially with France; "made Germany to perceive integration as the best way to ensure peace as well as economic development in a region" (Interview with Germany's GIZ official, Arusha, 7 May 2015). Several German leaders who visited the EAC pointed out in their speeches that Germany's integration experiences in the EU led the country to being a staunch supporter of integration more widely. For instance, Frank-Walter Steinmeier, who visited the EAC in November 2015 as Germany's Foreign Minister, stated in his speech that "Germany supports the EAC due to its own experience of European integration and out of deep conviction" (Auswärtiges Amt 2015). Moreover, the former President of Germany, Joachim Gauck, who visited the EAC in February 2015, also emphasised how Germany's experiences in the EU enabled the country to believe in supporting integration (Bundespräsidialamt 2015).

Beyond its positive encounters in the EU, Germany experienced division during the Cold War period between East and West Germany. That circumstance, according to a German diplomat, forced the country to experience the consequences of separation, thereby resulting in Germany's strong belief in supporting integration of different countries (Interview with German diplomat, Dar es Salaam, 27 April 2015). Additionally, the domestic experience of being a federal country made Germany believe in the importance of delegating some power to a national government or, in the case of integration, to a regional organisation (ibid.). Having elaborated all these experiences, the diplomat concluded by explaining how the German government believes that for African countries to achieve economic growth and development, regional integration is the best way forward (ibid.). In my interviews with EAC bureaucrats, some of them even cited Germany's unique experiences while explaining why the country is actively involved in supporting their integration process through its bilateral institutions (Interview with EAC official, Dar es Salaam, 30 April 2015; Interview with EAC official, Arusha, 8 May 2015).

Intentions to preserve Germany's unique identity in connection with how the country normally provides its foreign aid and how it is perceived in the region, could also explain why it has used bilateral institutions to support regionalism. As explained earlier, Germany's Federal Ministry for Economic Cooperation and Development, which coordinates foreign aid, typically separates its development assistance between financial and technical cooperation via different bilateral institutions. In this regard, Germany's usage of bilateral institutions could be part of preserving its identity in terms of how it manages its development assistance towards other parts of the world. However, the fact that Germany is actively involved in the EAC could be further explained by perceptions of the unique identity it established in the region. Earlier in this section we have seen how Germany started supporting the EAC in 1999 when the bloc was just reviving its integration process. Through this early involvement, Germany has established a unique identity in the region as one of the development partners that supported the EAC from its early days to the current era. As such, the country wishes to preserve that identity and has been involved in supporting regionalism projects via its own bilateral institutions throughout different phases. EAC bureaucrats also recognise Germany as the first European country that started supporting the bloc a long time ago (Interview with EAC official, Dar es Salaam, 30 April 2015; Interview with EAC official, Arusha, 8 May 2015). A major sign of close cooperation between Germany and the EAC can be seen through the physical presence of a GIZ office inside EAC's headquarters, whereas all other donor offices are situated outside the bloc's premises. According to an EAC official, the Community limits donor physical presence in its compound, but the GIZ has been allowed, due to its historical support of integration (Interview with EAC official, Arusha, 8 May 2015). Commenting on this close relationship with the EAC, a German diplomat said, "that is the reason why all other donor countries supporting integration in the region are envious of Germany" (Interview with German diplomat, Dar es Salaam, 27 April 2015).

The question that can additionally be asked in this section is whether other powerful states with the ability to use their bilateral institutions have internalised the integration norm and established unique identities in the EAC. Comparing France and the UK with Germany, the two have not had distinct national historical experiences, such as losing the Second World War, seeking to be integrated into the European community or separation of East and West during the Cold War. Those experiences, as explained earlier, have forced Germany to internalise the norm of integration to the extent of considering promotion of regionalism as an appropriate way of pursuing other national interests. Moreover, the two have not established unique identities of being promoters of regional integration since the early days of EAC's reestablishment as compared to the case of Germany. For Germany, being active in the EAC is not only about internalisation of integration norms, but also about preserving the unique identity of being an older partner when it comes to supporting regionalism. Maintaining that unique identity is the actual reason for Germany's active engagement in the EAC through its bilateral institutions. However, that has become possible due to other factors such as colonial ties, its state capacity as well as its strategic interests towards the region. Now let us move on to the other bilateral strategy of utilising a non-profit company, which is not used by Germany but employed by all other EU countries involved in supporting the EAC.

Use of a Non-Profit Company

The use of a non-profit company, TMEA, provides an opportunity for donors who are interested in supporting the EAC but might not have the wish or capacity to individually use their bilateral institutions in promoting integration. In this sense, donors with strong interests in the EAC can establish their own policy programmes and ask TMEA to implement them on their behalf. Additionally, development partners can generally contribute their funds to TMEA's activities, or even earmark the finances in specific sectors and programmes within the framework of the company. As a company, TMEA was established in 2010 as a not-for-profit instrument for Aid for Trade delivery in East Africa. Its focus is reflected in its name, TradeMark East Africa, which is a short form of trade and markets in East Africa. Currently, TMEA is funded by the development agencies of the following countries: Belgium, Canada, Denmark, Finland, France, Ireland, the Netherlands, Norway, the UK and the United States. Additionally, the EU joined TMEA as one of the donors in the financial year 2017/2018 (TMEA Annual Report 2017–2018:13).

TMEA was mainly initiated by the UK in 2009, and the other development partners joined to support the company's programmes (Hailey 2015). The company has offices in all EAC countries, and there is a regional office in Arusha, Tanzania, where the EAC headquarters is located. TMEA aims to promote regionalism at the national and regional levels, and as such, its country offices in the EAC partner states support integration projects at the domestic level, whereas the regional office is responsible for coordinating support at the wider EAC level. According to the UK's Department for International Development (DFID) official, TMEA aims to support integration at both levels because of its conviction that regional policies have to be implemented at the national level, so it is therefore "important to provide balanced support to both actors instead of only on one side of the equation at the regional level" (Interview with UK's DFID official, Dar es Salaam, 21 April 2015). In this context, the company works together with the EAC institutions, the EAC national governments, the private sector and civil society organisations to support trade integration in the region (TMEA Annual Report 2014–2015:5). In recent years, TMEA has expanded in EAC neighbouring countries and is implementing programmes across 13 nations in Eastern, Southern and the Horn of Africa. In addition to the seven EAC countries, TMEA implements programmes in Djibouti, Ethiopia, Malawi, Mozambique, Somaliland and Zambia (TMEA Annual Report 2020–2021:8).

The first phase of the TMEA programme started from 2010 to 2017, and the current, second, phase began in 2017 and is expected to end in 2023. By the year 2015, TMEA's secured fund totalled about GBP 401 million or USD 640 million (Personal Communication, UK's DFID official, 28 August 2015).[1] As illustrated in Table 5.7, the UK, under its bilateral development

---

1 The financial details on how donors finance the regional and country programmes is based on an internal document obtained from the UK Development agency (DFID) in Tanzania; that is why the secured amounts are in Pounds Sterling.

Table 5.7 Development Partners' Contributions to TMEA for Regional and Country Programmes, 2010–2015 (in Million Pounds Sterling)

TMEA Programme	Donor	Secured (£)
Regional/Core	DFID	74.3
	Denmark	15.8
	Netherlands	26.1
	Sweden	10.3
	Canada	6.9
	Finland	3.3
	USAID	15.7
Burundi	DFID	16.5
	Belgium	10.7
	USAID	0.6
Kenya	DFID	65.4
	Denmark	6.7
Rwanda	DFID	19.1
	USAID	3.6
	Sweden	4.2
	Belgium	4.3
South Sudan	DFID	7.1
Tanzania	DFID	55.4
	Sweden	2.8
	Belgium	2.6
Uganda	DFID	37.2
	Denmark	3.3
	Netherlands	6.3
	Sweden	3.2
TOTAL UK£		**401**

Source: Internal document of UK's DFID in Tanzania

agency, the DFID, was the major contributor, and it provided funding to all programmes at the regional and country level. Apart from Belgium, all other donors supported regional programmes together with a few selected country programmes. Belgium is the only donor which did not support regional programmes but financed only three country programmes: Burundi, Rwanda and Tanzania.

In the current second phase, TMEA continued to collect huge sums of funds from donor countries and by June 2021, it had accumulated a budget of approximately USD 1 billion (TMEA Annual Report 2020–2021:8). TMEA's work is currently driven by two main objectives: reducing barriers to trade and increased business competitiveness (ibid.). New donors, such as France and Ireland, which did not take part in the initial first phase of the programme, joined to support the activities of the company. Sweden, on the other hand, which supported TMEA's programme during its first phase, is no longer included in the list of donors currently involved in financing its activities. In this section, we explore why some EU countries chose the non-profit company in their bilateral support of regional integration in the EAC. As most of the donors are using TMEA, why then did Germany not prefer this model? In responding to these questions, foreign policy analysis approaches provide different answers.

Power-Based Approach

Powerful states, especially those with colonial ties, could also decide to actively use the non-profit company in their promotion of regional integration in the EAC. In that way, they can establish their own policy programmes and let TMEA implement them on their behalf. As shown earlier, the UK, which has colonial history in the region, initiated TMEA in 2009 and it is the biggest funder of its activities at the regional and national level. Before establishment of TMEA, the UK government also had its own regional programme, implemented by the DFID, known as the Regional East Africa Integration Programme, which began in 2008 (EAC Update e-newsletter 2008). After the establishment of TMEA, however, the programme was delegated to the company under its regional programme.

France, which does not have colonial ties with the EAC countries, on the other hand, participates in TMEA activities but less actively. The country only joined TMEA as a donor in 2021 and it does not support national-level programmes of EAC countries, but instead focuses on programmes directed to Horn of African countries mainly in Djibouti (TMEA Annual Report 2020–2021). Djibouti is a former French colony and was formerly known as French Somaliland. For this programme, the French development agency, the AFD, signed a EUR 29.9 million grant agreement with TMEA to support the development of the Djibouti corridor, which is considered the main trade route with Ethiopia (AFD 2021). The amount provided by France to TMEA partly came from the EU through its cooperation with the AFD and TMEA in the region (ibid.). The fact that France joined TMEA later, and that its focus is exclusively on its former colony of Djibouti, confirms how lack of direct colonial ties with EAC countries might have played a role in its decision to not actively use the company in supporting integration.

Although France and the UK use TMEA, whereby the latter with colonial ties is more active than the former without such connections with the EAC countries, neorealists consider the importance of security concerns in powerful countries' decisions. Direct pursuit of security interests via TMEA might not be possible due to the company's focus on trade-related activities. In that sense, security-related projects can rarely be found within the framework of TMEA, unless we consider trade promotion as an indirect way of supporting peace. That would, however, mean adopting a liberalist approach that is contrary to the logic of the neorealist understanding applied in this section. Furthermore, as argued in the previous section, France and the UK prefer to deal with their security concerns in Africa within the framework of the United Nations Security Council, and thus they do not need TMEA to pursue their strategic ambitions in the region. The question then remains as to why Germany is not using TMEA in its support to the EAC. In responding to that question, a German diplomat claimed that it would not add much value to the company if another donor joined it, adding that, "Germany prefers to continue with its capacity building programmes that enabled it to build a close relationship with the EAC" (Personal Communication, German diplomat, 10 November 2015).

Interest-Based Approach

Countries which benefit economically from the EAC have been expected to choose or actively use TMEA in their support of integration. Assessing economic benefits through trade, as we saw earlier in the case of France, Germany and the UK, countries in the EAC are not important trading partners to them as compared to Nigeria and South Africa. As neoliberal institutionalism considers all states, regardless of their power position, to be concerned with economic benefits, in this section we examine another case of a trade relationship between the EAC countries and a less powerful EU country. The aim is to assess whether there exist strong economic linkages with less powerful donor countries that could explain their decision to choose a non-profit company in their regionalism support. The Netherlands, as a unique case that exclusively supports the EAC via TMEA only, has been selected in this context as a representative example for less powerful EU countries. Tables 5.8 and 5.9 show that the Netherlands also does not trade much with EAC countries but more with Nigeria and South Africa.

These findings show that current economic benefits do not explain states' decisions to choose TMEA. However, countries might anticipate gaining economically from the EAC in the future when the region becomes more thoroughly integrated. As argued earlier, that argument follows an ideational logic of regarding regionalism promotion as the best way of pursuing future commercial gains. The Dutch government, for instance, has shown its interests in combining trade and development policy, specifically with shifting towards trade over development. In its policy agenda "A World to Gain: A New Agenda for Aid, Trade and Investment," the government expresses its interest in using aid mainly to bolster trade in different parts of the world as a way of gaining future economic opportunities (Ministry of Foreign Affairs of the Netherlands 2013). Furthermore, in its new policy document for foreign trade and development cooperation titled "Do what we do best," the Dutch government emphasised a win–win situation in its development cooperation through supporting sectors that also present opportunities for the Dutch business community (Ministry of Foreign Affairs of the Netherlands 2022:46). Taking all these factors into consideration, TMEA could provide an opportunity for the Netherlands to focus on financing sectors in the EAC that might

Table 5.8 Dutch Exports and Imports to and from EAC countries, 2010–2014 (in Million US Dollars)

	Exports					Imports				
	Tanzania	Kenya	Uganda	Rwanda	Burundi	Tanzania	Kenya	Uganda	Rwanda	Burundi
2010	128.36	224.50	59.86	19.27	4.18	104.16	327.45	115.49	0.13	0.65
2011	188.52	250.37	59.73	39.53	6.03	112.87	365.18	125.51	1.61	0.81
2012	147.67	206.09	73.68	56.28	8.56	110.36	361.77	106.55	1.45	0.96
2013	200.52	282.69	90.37	56.62	13.81	113.25	372.68	99.38	0.85	0.18
2014	155.35	210.17	77.10	39.15	26.03	90.60	455.40	116.60	1.21	0.81

Source: IMF Direction of Trade Statistics (DOTS)

Table 5.9 Dutch Exports and Imports to and from Sub-Saharan Africa, South Africa and Nigeria, 2010–2014 (in Million US Dollars)

	Exports			Imports		
	SSA	*South Africa*	*Nigeria*	*SSA*	*South Africa*	*Nigeria*
2010	11,080.57	2,355.06	4,495.83	11,952.27	2,766.98	3,169.83
2011	13,967.15	2,823.23	5,365.18	15,631.20	3,203.35	5,109.08
2012	12,482.34	3,155.24	3,478.89	19,878.01	2,864.40	10,026.23
2013	13,858.68	2,930.50	3,554.37	17,610.39	3,270.07	7,522.01
2014	13,768.23	2,676.56	3,509.11	18,991.08	3,390.08	8,700.42

Source: IMF Direction of Trade Statistics (DOTS)

benefit Dutch businesses. Those sectors of interest in the EAC, according to a Dutch diplomat, include financing TMEA programmes to support development of infrastructure, as well as training and supportive information and communications technology (Personal Communication, Dutch diplomat, 10 November 2015).

Other less powerful EU countries are also interested in maintaining close strategic relationships with individual EAC countries, and as such, they use TMEA to support specific national programmes. That has been the case with Belgium, which uses TMEA mainly to support country programmes of its former colonies of Rwanda and Burundi. "As a small donor with few resources it's not feasible to use our national development agency to support integration," said a Belgian diplomat, adding that their focus is to support TMEA's country programmes of their former colonies of Burundi and Rwanda, due to their strategic importance to Belgium (Interview with Belgian diplomat, Dar es Salaam, 22 April 2015). As shown in Table 5.7, in addition to Burundi and Rwanda, Belgium also supported the Tanzanian country programme. This is probably a strategic choice due to the Dar es Salaam port project sponsored by TMEA, whereby most of the imports and exports of Rwanda and Burundi – due to the countries being landlocked – go through the Port of Dar es Salaam in Tanzania (World Bank 2013:31). Financing the Tanzanian country programme could be considered an indirect form of Belgium's support to Burundi and Rwanda. When those former colonies are well integrated in the EAC, Belgian businesses could also benefit through large regional markets for their exports and investments. Examples provided in this section show how less powerful countries can also use the non-profit company to support projects that might benefit their business communities in the future.

Norm/Identity-Based Approach

States which chose the non-profit company are expected to regard that strategy as an effective and appropriate way of supporting regional economic integration. This is because TMEA focuses mainly on implementing economic-related activities and programmes, and some donors might regard the company's approach as the best way to support regionalism in the EAC. However, as all activities within the non-profit company are implemented by TMEA on behalf of donors, it would be difficult for states to preserve their unique identity in the region. That would mainly be possible if they directly engaged with the EAC via their national bilateral development agencies. In this sense, selection of the non-profit company can mainly be explained by a normative understanding of what states believe is the best way of supporting economic integration and of pursuing their interests in an appropriate manner.

TMEA's strategy of supporting integration at the regional and national levels has been regarded by donor countries as an effective way of promoting regionalism, as it gives them the flexibility to choose different projects of interest across different areas. Donors can also establish their own projects and ask TMEA to implement them on their behalf. Denmark is an example of a less powerful EU country that established its own regional policy programme and delegated it to TMEA. That Danish programme titled "Regional Economic Integration Support Programme" started in 2012 and ended in 2015. According to its programme officer, the government did not want to earmark its support to specific projects, but it wanted TMEA to use the finances to support various regional projects to boost economic integration in the EAC (Interview with Danish programme official, Dar es Salaam, 28 April 2015). For Denmark "as a small country that also benefited from the EU," said a Danish programme consultant, "its promotion of economic integration via TMEA is based on its belief that the more integrated the region is, the better its able to address some of the challenges of development whether infrastructure challenges, whether limited markets, et cetera" (Interview with Danish programme consultant, Arusha, 7 May 2015). The possibility of financing different trade-related projects has been an added value of TMEA to the donors. The Danish programme official emphasised this advantage, arguing that "the company is more attractive to other donors because it focuses on projects with tangible results that are readily visible" (Interview with Danish programme official, Dar es Salaam, 28 April 2015).

In addition to Demark, all other officials involved in supporting the EAC via TMEA regard the company's initiatives as the best and most effective way of fostering economic integration. The UK, as shown earlier, also established its own policy programme in 2008 and delegated it to TMEA when the company was established in 2010. According to the UK's DFID official, "the UK wanted something different, not the traditional way of giving budget support, but rather facilitating integration at regional and country level" (Interview with UK's DFID official, Dar es Salaam, 21 April 2015). Even the case of the Netherlands, which we explored in the previous section, seems to regard TMEA as the most effective way of promoting regional economic integration in the EAC. "Our focus will remain on the implementation side of regional economic integration through the TMEA," claimed a Dutch diplomat (Personal Communication, Dutch diplomat, 10 November 2015). Belgium, on the other hand, though it mainly supported its former colonies through TMEA country programmes; its diplomat also gave a normative statement for the country's usage of the non-profit company, arguing that Burundi and Rwanda are landlocked countries and that is why they support their integration in the EAC through TMEA (Interview with Belgian diplomat, Dar es Salaam, 22 April 2015).

Most of the donors regard using the non-profit company as the best way of supporting economic integration in the region as they can choose to finance different projects or even establish their own regional policy programmes and delegate them to the company. TMEA then becomes not only an effective instrument to promote economic integration, but also an appropriate means of pursuing their interests in the region. This, in connection with other factors, such as their state capacities, colonial ties and other unique interests, determine whether states actively use TMEA or only contribute to its activities. In the following section, we move on to the final bilateral strategy of contributing to the Partnership Fund, which has been chosen by most of the donor countries.

Use of Partnership Fund

Through the EAC Partnership Fund, donor countries are able to contribute their finances in a basket fund in order to support EAC projects and programmes. The fund was established in 2006 with the aim of coordinating donors in their financing of EAC integration projects (EAC Secretariat 2013:9). It is governed by a Memorandum of Understanding (MoU) signed by the EAC and the development partners contributing to the EAC Partnership Fund. Paragraph 5 of the MoU describes two overall objectives of the fund, including enhancing regional integration and socio-economic development of the EAC, as well as facilitating the harmonisation and alignment of development partners' support to the region (EAC 2013a). In paragraph 7, the MoU clarifies further how the fund is coordinated by a steering committee which consists of one representative from the EAC, one from each development partner contributing to the fund, and any other member who may be designated by the committee (ibid.). This paragraph also describes the function of the steering committee which involves monitoring and supervising the fund; giving strategic and policy guidance regarding the management of the fund; considering and approving all projects, work plans, budgets and other activities to be financed through the fund; as well as considering and approving progress reports, financial reports and external audit reports (ibid.).

With the Partnership Fund, development partners contribute their finances to a basket fund and the EAC has some control in managing and financing different integration activities. From the inception of the fund in 2006 until financial year 2014/15, a total of USD 48 million has been disbursed by donors (EAC 2022b). Donor members of the Partnership Fund include Belgium, Canada, Denmark, Finland, France, Germany, Japan, Norway, Sweden, the United Kingdom and the European Union (ibid.). In addition, the fund has one non-contributing member, the World Bank and four observers: Australia, Italy, Switzerland and Turkey (ibid.). Table 5.10 shows contributions of development partners to the fund until the financial year 2013/14.

The last financial disbursement from donor countries to the EAC Partnership Fund was a budget of USD 6.9 million in the financial year 2014/2015 (EAC 2022b). This budget was intended to support integration activities in four key priority areas: (i) implementation of the EAC Common Market Protocol and Customs Union Protocol; (ii) support to the implementation of the East African Monetary Union; (iii) enhancing public awareness

Table 5.10 Contributions of the Partnership Fund in USD (FY 2006/2007 to FY 2013/2014)

Development Partner	FY 2006/2007	FY 2007/2008	FY 2008/2009	FY 2009/2010	FY 2010/2011	FY 2011/2012	FY 2012/2013	FY 2013/2014	TOTAL
Belgium	0	0	391,774	0	380,969	0	0	600,768.30	1,373,511.3
Canada	0	0	788,395	928,359	1,004,296	0	0	0	2,721,050
Denmark	0	768,795	625,717	238,095	0	525,394	1,622,129.58	1,085,187.19	4,865,317.77
Finland	0	0	1,901,695	898,800	1,300,000	1,267,000	0	1,340,600.00	6,708,095
France	0	0	129,870	0	13,889	0	23,333.33	27,753.42	194,845.75
Germany	394,695	395,655	700,935	761,115	1,335,980	976,005.	1,638,755	0	6,203,140
Japan	0	0	0	0	21,000	21,000	17,853.00	0	59,853
Norway	246,225	278,319	507,828	256,279	0	0	1,799,422.75	1,613,033	4,681,106.75
Sweden	0	480,240	383,430	414,030	1,345,142	1,014,439.97	1,050,560	1,047,410	5,735,251.97
UK (DFID)	0	0	1,181,500	2,730,200	2,613,750	1,368,500	0	0	7,893,950
Total	**640,920**	**1,923,009**	**6,611,144**	**6,226,878**	**8,015,026**	**5,172,338.97**	**6,132,053.66**	**5,714,751.91**	**40,436,121.54**

Source: EAC Partnership Fund Annual Report FY 2013/2014

and popular participation in the EAC; and (iv) capacity-strengthening of the EAC (EAC 2014). Though donor countries could contribute to the fund and support all those projects, most of them preferred to additionally support the EAC through either use of their national bilateral institutions or the non-profit company. So, the question arising here is why EU countries donated to the EAC Partnership Fund in addition to their other bilateral channels of interest. The unique cases of Ireland and the Netherlands will also be explored, especially as they are the only countries that did not join the Partnership Fund in their engagement with the EAC. As we will see, foreign policy approaches, especially power and interest-based perspectives, regard the fund as an additional tool to pursue states' interests, whereas the norms/identity approach considers complying with the donor coordination norm to be the main reason for states' selection of the fund.

Power-Based Approach

As powerful EU states have huge financial resources, it is expected that they would also contribute to the Partnership Fund in addition to their other bilateral channels of interest. This could be a strategy for them to maximise their influence in the region by engaging in all possible channels of supporting regional integration. When powerful countries are involved in the steering committee that coordinates the fund, they can use their influence in promoting their interests, even within the basket fund. As explained earlier, within the steering committee, donors approve, monitor and also supervise the fund, and that is an additional opportunity for powerful countries to use their positions of power to advance their agendas in the region in coordination with other donor countries involved in the Partnership Fund.

Germany, for instance, has been contributing to the fund since its inception in 2006. According to a GIZ official, it was Germany, together with Norway, that invented the fund (Interview with Germany's GIZ official, Arusha, 7 May 2015). An EAC official also regarded Germany as one of the masterminds of the Partnership Fund, arguing that the country did not want the EAC to ask for aid in a piecemeal way, and that is why "they organised all donors to put together their money in a basket" (Interview with EAC official, Arusha, 8 May 2015). On the other hand, France and the UK joined the EAC Partnership Fund beginning in the financial year 2008/2009. Both Germany and the UK, which have colonial ties with EAC countries, contributed more to the fund compared to France. Until the financial year 2013/2014, Germany and the UK donated around USD 6.2 million and USD 7.9 million respectively, whereas France contributed approximately USD 195,000 (see again Table 5.10 showing development partners' contributions to the fund).

Such huge payments by powerful countries, especially with colonial history, could explain their need to seek further influence in their engagements with the EAC. Neorealism, however, regards powerful countries as being concerned with their security interests, and, in the context of the Partnership Fund, it is not clear how such preferences can be pursued. That is because the typical financed projects elaborated earlier in this section do not deal with security-related activities in the region. In this sense, the fund can simply be regarded as an additional channel for influence, but if states want to deal with their security concerns, they can use their other bilateral channels through which they can directly support projects of interest.

Interest-Based Approach

Other donors, for instance less powerful countries, can also use the Partnership Fund in addition to their involvement in other bilateral channels. They might not be seeking influence, as it has been suggested powerful states do, but rather they can maintain friendly relationships with a region that offers them economic benefits. However, as we saw in previous sections, the current economic benefit measured through trade cannot explain states' motivation unless we consider future commercial gains. Most of the countries involved in supporting the EAC have been shown to also expect future benefits for their business communities, especially given their involvement in supporting economic integration activities. Among typical activities financed through the fund, initiatives related to economic integration are involved, such as implementation of a customs union, a common market and monetary union protocols.

Less powerful countries without huge capacities to engage directly with the EAC could also benefit from contributing to the Partnership Fund through their participation in the steering committee that coordinates the fund. As explained earlier, the committee brings together all donor members of the EAC in different phases of monitoring, supervising and management of the fund. Paragraph 8 of the MoU demonstrates that the steering committee must meet at least twice a year to perform these functions (EAC 2013a). According to a Belgian diplomat, it is easier for them "as a small donor to get a lot of dialogue with the EAC through those Steering Committee meetings" (Interview with Belgian diplomat, Dar es Salaam, 22 April 2015). As the EAC has some sort of control over the funds in terms of managing and financing projects, it is also committed to the fund and would like donors to contribute more to the EAC Partnership Fund than to their own bilateral projects (Interview with EAC official, Arusha, 8 May 2015). In this context, the Partnership Fund can be considered an instrument whereby donor countries can also symbolically demonstrate to the EAC that they are concerned with its integration progress.

Though there are additional interests, some states could gain through their involvement in the fund; EU countries such as Ireland and the Netherlands did not join it in their support of integration in the EAC. In the case of Ireland, the country was rather late joining a group of donors that supported the EAC via TMEA, starting from the financial year 2017/2018 (TMEA Annual Report 2017–2018:13). This was already after the last disbursement of donors to the

Partnership Fund, which occurred in the financial year 2014/2015. However, the case of the Netherlands is curious as it started supporting the EAC during the first phase of TMEA, and yet ignored joining the Partnership Fund. Responding to why the country made that decision, the Dutch diplomat argued that the Netherlands is not interested in supporting the EAC directly but focuses rather on the implementation side of regional economic integration through TMEA (Personal Communication, Dutch diplomat, 10 November 2015). This shows that the Netherlands is clear about its interests in economic integration in the region, and it does not need to pursue other friendlier, symbolic approaches towards the EAC as is the case with other donors.

Norm/Identity-Based Approach

One of the key elements in the Partnership Fund is the possibility of coordinating donor countries, as they all contribute to a basket fund without earmarking their finances to different projects. In that way, donors have to agree together, within the steering committee, on what projects to finance and the EAC takes control of their implementation. That is why constructivists regard the EAC Partnership Fund from an ideational point of view, whereby states intend to comply to the donor coordination norm. As explained in the previous chapter, donor coordination has been regarded internationally as the best way of ensuring aid effectiveness. As the Partnership Fund offers the opportunity for donors to coordinate among themselves, it is expected that states will choose the fund to signal that they comply with that international norm and thereby achieve an identity of being concerned with donor coordination and aid effectiveness.

Complying to that identity can be seen symbolically in the way donors contribute to the fund but also engage in other bilateral channels of their interests. In fact, some donor countries believe that the EAC Partnership Fund is being mismanaged by the EAC (Interview with German diplomat, Dar es Salaam, 27 April 2015; Interview with Belgian diplomat, Dar es Salaam, 22 April 2015). Despite such perceptions of the EAC, donors continued to donate to the basket fund until the financial year 2014/2015. When I asked an EAC official about why there were no financial disbursements from donors in the following years, he claimed that the fund had been disbanded by the donors (Personal Communication, EAC official, 11 November 2022). This was because, according to the EAC official, "they wanted to support projects directly rather than putting money in the basket" (ibid.). Scepticism about the EAC's management of the fund was also the reason why the EU joined the EAC Partnership Fund, but it did not give money directly to the EAC; instead, it directly financed those projects agreed to within the fund (Interview with EU diplomat, Dar es Salaam, 24 April 2015).

When the fund was initiated by Germany and Norway back in 2006, its aim was to coordinate donor finances targeted at the EAC. As such, it attracted many donors as they saw it as an opportunity to comply with the donor coordination norm. Even when the EAC was promoting the fund and asking other donors to join, the bloc emphasised the fund's role of coordinating donors in their promotion of its integration (EAC 2016). This helped various donors to join the fund, with the exception of a few countries such as the Netherlands, which decided to exclusively focus on regional economic integration through TMEA. As donors contributed to the fund until the financial year 2014/2015, this clearly shows that the need to comply with the donor coordination norm at the recipient level might be jettisoned, especially if there is mismanagement of the finances.

Bilateral Promotion of Integration

Through states' bilateral promotion of regional integration outside the EU, we see that there are different factors that could explain why donor countries prefer certain strategies in their interactions with the EAC. Different variables from foreign policy approaches, including power positions, interests as well as norms/identity, have been used to elucidate states' decisions on why they support the EAC via their bilateral institutions, a non-profit company, or the Partnership Fund. Each of these approaches has its own strengths and weaknesses in explaining the situation in the EAC. Some decisions can be better explained by one foreign policy approach rather than another, and there are circumstances where theoretical perspectives with different ontological assumptions can be combined to explain a specific outcome. To systematically analyse the situation and avoid an overdetermined argument in the sense that more than one variable explains an outcome, in this section I will categorise the importance of each theoretical approach in explaining states' decisions. This is done by separating factors that can be regarded to have caused the actual outcome from those which might have provided sufficient conditions for the results.

The use of bilateral institutions, a strategy mainly employed by Germany, has been effectively explained by power- and norm/identity-based approaches and to a lesser extent by an interest-based perspective. As one of the most powerful EU countries with colonial ties in the region, Germany adopted a strong interest in supporting the EAC via its national development agencies. Through that strategy, Germany has been able to pursue its security interests in the region by establishing and supporting security-related regional programmes in addition to projects in other sectors. On the other hand, Germany's internalisation of integration norms based on its national experience and its intention to preserve a unique identity in the EAC as the oldest supporter of integration, have motivated the country to actively support the bloc via its own bilateral institutions. Economic interests measured through trade earnings, however, could not explain Germany's decision since it trades more with Nigeria and South Africa than with EAC countries, and as such, commercial gains can only be regarded in terms of future prospects. In this regard, the actual reason for Germany's decision is based on the norm/identity approach, specifically its aim of preserving its unique identity as one of the first supporters of integration in the EAC. However, the sufficient conditions for such an outcome are centred on the power-based approach given Germany's capacity to use its national institutions in the region, its colonial ties with some countries in the EAC bloc, and its aim to pursue security interests via regional organisations. Comparing Germany, and other powerful countries which can fulfil some of those sufficient conditions, it becomes clear that preserving a unique identity in the region has not been a major concern for France or the UK.

The use of the non-profit company, TMEA, which has been employed by several EU member states, could also be effectively explained by the norm/identity approach and partly by the power-based perspective. With the interest-based approach, as argued previously, the assumptions would hold if we examined potential future economic gains, as most of the states using TMEA also trade more with Nigeria and South Africa than with EAC countries. The norm/identity approach, in this context, has clearly shown how those donors with strong beliefs in the importance of economic integration consider supporting the EAC via TMEA as the most appropriate and best way of engaging with the EAC as well as of pursuing their future economic gains in the region. Some variables from the power-based approach, specifically colonial ties and state capacity, provide sufficient conditions for whether states actively use TMEA or not. This could explain why a former colonial power with high capacity, such as the UK, was able to actively initiate TMEA and finance most of its projects, while a small donor, such as Belgium, with less capacity, can also actively use TMEA, mainly to support its former colonies.

The use of the Partnership Fund was, rather, an extra bilateral channel for donors to engage with the EAC in addition to their other channels of interest. The norm/identity approach could better explain why donor countries chose the fund, given the importance of complying with the donor coordination norm. As a result, states continued to contribute to the fund until the financial year 2014/2015, despite their scepticism that the fund was being mismanaged by the EAC. In addition, the power-based approach provided some variables such as colonial history and state capacity, which could be considered to be sufficient conditions in explaining why former colonies such as Germany and the UK might have contributed huge amounts to the fund as compared to France.

This chapter shows that states' selection of bilateral strategies to promote regional integration can be explained by different foreign policy approaches. It is the norm/identity-based approach that has the highest explanatory power, and its variables can mainly be regarded as actual causes of states' decisions. On the other hand, the power-based approach can partly explain the situation, especially by providing variables that are considered to be sufficient conditions for the outcome. The interest-based approach, however, has the lowest explanatory power as trade connections between the EAC member states and donor countries are rather low; therefore, commercial interests are regarded only in terms of the possibility of future gains. The argument about future economic gains strengthens even further the norm/identity approach in explaining the outcome, as constructivists would regard this as an ideational goal rather than a material concern motivated by current commercial benefits. These empirical findings show that what determines states' choices in their bilateral promotion of regional integration is first and foremost what they consider to be appropriate in pursuing their interests, based on their norms and identity. However, their choices of strategies depend on other factors such as their capacities, historical ties and their focal interests in a specific region. As EU member states can bilaterally engage with other regions outside the EU context, this may cause various effects in those recipient regional organisations. In the next part of this book, we will see how those effects could be experienced in the EAC.

Part III
Effects in East Africa

6 Donor Coordination and Proliferation

Now that we've explored why the EU and its member states are supporting regional integration through multilateral and bilateral channels, let us move on to assess the effects of such differentiated engagements in the EAC. Discussions on foreign aid have always been linked to the need to ensure donor coordination, especially in the current era of donor proliferation, whereby there is an increase in sources and channels of aid directed towards recipients as opposed to the actual volume of aid itself (Acharya et al. 2006:1). The problem of donor proliferation started to emerge as early as the 1960s, and the need to coordinate donor activities was one of the reasons for the creation of the Development Assistance Committee (DAC) of the Organisation for Economic Co-operation and Development (OECD) in 1961 (Herman 2013:10). Although DAC members played a central role in post-war aid systems, in recent years there are other, non-DAC, donors who also provide aid. With these developments, aid can spread among several instruments and interventions per donor and consequently lead to the problems of donor proliferation (Acharya et al. 2006:1).

The EU and its member states also regard aid proliferation as a serious problem, and they have engaged in various international initiatives to ensure aid effectiveness. Such initiatives have been discussed in four different high-level forums, including the Rome High Level Forum in 2003, the Paris Declaration in 2005 and the subsequent forums in Accra (2008) and Busan (2011). During the Paris Declaration in 2005, a document was produced setting out five different principles to ensure aid effectiveness, which include: (i) ownership by recipient countries; (ii) alignment of donor aid with recipient objectives; (iii) harmonisation of donors' systems; (iv) managing results to improve decision-making; and (v) mutual accountability for development results. The EU was involved in all these high-level forums, and it has been argued that some of the donor coordination principles agreed during the Paris Declaration were highly influenced by the EU (Carbone 2013:346). Such developments have made some scholars consider the EU as a potential donor-coordinating actor when it comes to the topic of foreign aid (Carbone 2013; Mürle 2007; Schulz 2007).

DOI: 10.4324/9781003290155-9

Given such donor coordination initiatives by the EU and its member states to ensure aid effectiveness, the case of the EAC provides an opportunity to assess whether Europe practises what it preaches. In this sense, various questions related to the effects of European initiatives in the EAC could be asked: for instance, whether their regional aid is coordinated. Moreover, as briefly mentioned earlier, some literature argues for EU actorness when it comes to foreign aid, so a follow-up question based on such arguments is whether the EU is perceived as a coordinating actor in the EAC. Finally is the question of whether there are challenges experienced by EAC regional actors caused by proliferated activities of European regional aid. Before answering these questions related to the effects of European initiatives in the EAC in Chapter 7, this chapter starts by explaining how donor coordination and proliferation will be examined. First, we are going to explore how regional aid is defined in the context of this book as well as the sectors and projects that can be supported through such assistance. Afterwards, I move on to explain how donor coordination and proliferation will be analysed, followed by a final section on data analysis.

Regional Aid Sectors and Projects

Regional integration occurs when a group of neighbouring countries transfer at least some authority and sovereignty rights to the regional level (Nye 1968; Lindberg 1970). Through this process, neighbouring countries can establish cooperative relations with each other in different policy areas. A regional organisation such as the EAC, which has different scopes and areas of cooperation in different policy fields, is classified in the literature as a "general purpose organisation" (Lenz et al. 2015). In such an organisation, there are different areas of cooperation that can also attract donor countries to engage in supporting different sectors of regional integration processes. Regional aid is different from the classical assistance towards recipient countries that focuses on individual nations. With regional aid, the recipients are a group of countries within the framework of their regional organisations. Regional aid is intended to support sectors and projects that could facilitate integration among countries within a specific region (Engel and Mattheis 2020; Söderbaum and Brolin 2016; Gray 2011; Jolliff 2015). Regional organisations are quite new types of aid recipients even in the analyses of development cooperation literature as compared to foreign aid towards recipient countries (Jolliff 2015:1–2). In this section, I identify five different sectors that are more likely to be supported by donors through their regional aid initiatives. These sectors are based on what are regarded as being typical areas of cooperation in the literature of regional integration, but also on what donor countries and recipient regional organisations consider essential in supporting integration processes.

Regional economic integration is one of the key sectors that is being pursued by many regional organisations around the world. In Europe, for instance, advancing economic integration among countries was regarded as the best way to attain peace in the continent after the end of the Second World War. This functionalist approach towards integration assumed that there was a need to build peace around common needs and functions in order to unite people across state borders (Mitrany 1943). Neofunctionalists took those arguments further by emphasising the role of a spill-over effect, especially in the economic sector, in creating strong incentives for integration in other areas (Haas 1964). In other parts of the world, for instance in African countries, seeking economic integration after independence was not a strategy towards seeking peace, as it was in Europe, but rather to facilitate economic development and state formation (Axline 1977). On the other hand, the theory of economic integration is not concerned with the reasons why countries pursue economic cooperation itself, but it outlines five stages of integration from the shallowest to the deepest level: at the shallowest stage is the preferential trade area (PTA) between two or more countries that agree to reduce tariffs for certain products; a free trade area (FTA) is a PTA in which all barriers to trade are eliminated; customs unions are FTAs with a common external tariff; a common market goes further to allow not only free movement of goods, but also services, capital and labour; and the final and the deepest stage of economic integration is economic union, which combines a common market with a monetary union (Balassa 1973). The EAC also follows some stages of economic integration theory, and it established its customs union in 2005 and a common market in 2010. In 2013, the EAC member states signed the protocol to establish a monetary union. Such economic integration policies pursued by the EAC might attract donor countries to support trade-related activities as a means of facilitating economic cooperation in the region. Subsequently, economic growth at the regional level may also end up benefiting donor countries themselves, for instance by getting large markets for their exports and investments.

Regional security is another major sector that can be pursued by a group of countries through their regional organisations. This might happen especially when there are perceived security threats in some countries in the region that could affect other neighbouring countries, for instance, in the form of waves of refugees and spill-over of domestic instability across borders. Some African regional organisations, such as the ECOWAS, have been highly studied in the way they deal with security threats at the regional level through solving regional conflicts, combating proliferation of small arms and fighting against international terrorist networks (Francis 2005; Iheduru 2011). The EAC is also concerned with its security in the region, and its member states signed a peace and security protocol in 2013 that identified various objectives for fostering regional peace and security. Some of those objectives include combating terrorism and piracy; peace support operations; prevention of genocide; disaster management and crisis response; management of refugees; control of proliferation of small arms and light weapons; and combating transnational and cross-border crimes (EAC 2013b). With such ambitions, donor countries could consider the EAC to be a strategic partner in dealing with security challenges, thereby working with the bloc to promote peace in the region. After all, insecurity in these regions could also have negative externalities in their own countries, for instance through illegal migration and flows of refugees.

Different regional institutions could also be established within a specific region so as to facilitate integration further. As regional organisations receive their mandate from sovereign member states, various institutions could be introduced to enforce and implement regionally agreed policies. This, according to international relations scholars, is important, especially in ensuring credible commitments among states when they cooperate in this anarchical world (Axelrod and Keohane 1986). Today, most regional organisations have secretariats which have responsibilities such as agenda setting and implementation of daily regional administrative tasks. Regional parliaments have also been established to facilitate clear decision-making procedures as well as regional courts to settle regional disputes. The EAC has also created such institutions and considers, for instance, the secretariat, regional parliaments and courts as among the main organs of their integration process (EAC 2022c). The secretariat of the EAC is the executive organ that implements regulations and directives adopted by the Council; the court known as the East African Court of Justice (EACJ) is the judicial organ of the Community that ensures adherence to the law in the interpretation and application of compliance with the EAC Treaty; the regional parliament called the East African Legislative Assembly (EALA) is the legislative organ with a cardinal function to further EAC objectives, through its legislative, representative and oversight mandate (ibid.). Given the major tasks with which some EAC major regional institutions are mandated, donor countries are likely to engage in supporting their work towards realisation of integration in the region.

Regional non-state actors can also play an essential role in regional integration processes. Such actors can involve businesses, firms, interest groups and non-governmental organisations (NGOs), whose activities beyond their national borders could facilitate further integration processes. Non-state actors are regarded as transactors due to their engagement in various forms of transactions, such as through seeking to exchange "goods, services, ideas, information, or funds across national frontiers" (Sandholtz and Stone Sweet 2013:4). The activities of non-state actors can lead to a process that has been dubbed regionalisation in the sense of "the growth of societal integration within a region and the often undirected social and economic interaction" (Hurrell 1995:39). Given the importance of non-state actors in the process of regional integration, donor countries are interested in supporting them to facilitate their regional involvement. One of the main objectives of the Treaty for the Establishment of the East African Community is to enhance and strengthen "partnerships with the private sector and civil society in order to achieve sustainable socio-economic and political development" (Article 5, Section 3g). When donor countries support non-state actors, it is also a strategic move towards reinforcing other sectors of integration as well. Projects to foster economic integration, for instance, also constitute assisting business actors and the private sector to engage in trade and investment beyond their national borders. Even promotion of security might involve funding the work of different interest groups and NGOs to foster peace in the region.

Member states themselves might also be key actors supported by donor countries to fully engage in implementing their agreed regional policies. As regional organisations bring together states with different capacities, this can affect the way they engage with regional policies. A regional economic integration policy such as a common market, for instance, requires states to harmonise their rules to allow for free movement of goods, services, capital and labour. In this context, public and private actors in countries with more capable states might be more effective in implementing those economic regulations as compared with countries with weaker states (Bruszt and Campos 2019:450). The EAC also brings together countries with different state capacities and this could affect the way these nations implement and adopt regional policies. Some countries, such as Kenya, Tanzania and Uganda, are founding members of the EAC; therefore, they might be more experienced in adopting regional policies compared to new member states. With these differences in terms of state capacities, donor countries may direct their regional aid towards supporting individual EAC countries in coping with integration processes in the region. Through supporting member states, donors can also maintain their special relations with individual countries through aid that is aimed at boosting their involvement in regional integration.

The five regional sectors analysed in this section, involving regional economic integration, security, institutions, non-state actors and capacity-building in member states, are based on regional integration literature as well as what might be regarded as essential in terms of integration by the EAC and donor countries. Given the importance of those regional sectors, donor countries are more likely to introduce or support various activities in these different areas. In this sense, it is necessary for donors to coordinate between each other, especially if they are interested in supporting projects in similar sectors.

Donor Coordination Analysis

For a long time, lack of aid coordination has been identified as a serious problem facing recipient countries. More than 30 years ago, scholars started linking the lack of aid coordination with the failure of African countries to make use of their development assistance effectively (Whittington and Calhoun 1988:296). Although most of such studies have been employed to assess classical aid to recipient countries, such challenges can also occur in the new type of aid to promote integration aimed at regional organisations. As European countries are interested in promoting integration via different channels, the question of how they coordinate themselves becomes relevant, especially when they are all interested in supporting similar regional sectors and projects.

Literature shows that donor coordination can partly occur when development partners are pursuing different channels to provide their aid to recipients. Klingebiel et al. (2017:146–147), for instance, use the term "degrees of coordination" to explain how donors can pursue coordination in different ways: from the lowest, which constitutes simply exchange of information; to partial harmonisation of strategies and approaches; to the most ambitious degree of fully integrating activities. Applying a similar assessment to the way the EU and its member states engage with the EAC, it becomes clear that European initiatives are not fully integrated; however, there are partial harmonisation mechanisms being employed in the region; for instance, co-financing, whereby donors are discouraged from establishing their own projects in sectors which are supported by other donors but instead are encouraged to contribute their finances to those existing initiatives. In this context, the principle of a lead donor can be employed in recipient countries or regional organisations to ensure that specific donor countries are taking the lead in financing particular sectors (Knack and Rahman 2004:26). Akin to this is the strategy of specialisation that requires a donor to pick a certain sector in which it would like to specialise and commit its resources in that area rather than spreading their finances across different sectors (Knack et al. 2011:1910). In this way, other donors, which are not leading or specialising in specific sectors, can co-finance activities in those areas which are led by other donors, or they can also match their activities in connection to other donor projects to avoid duplication.

The question of the EU's ability to coordinate its member states also becomes relevant, especially when countries also prefer to use other bilateral channels to support integration. As we saw in the introduction to this chapter, the EU has been highly involved in various high-level international forums to promote donor coordination. For instance, in 2006, the EU had already begun initiatives to coordinate its aid internally with its member states, through a declaration called the European Consensus on Development. This led to further developments in 2007, whereby the EU adopted its own Code of Conduct on Complementarity and Division of Labour. The Code of Conduct aimed to urge member states to, among other things, focus their aid on fewer countries and on sectors where they had a comparative advantage. The emphasis on the EU's internal coordination to ensure aid effectiveness was even declared again in another document, the Operational Framework on Aid Effectiveness, adopted in 2009 and revised in 2011. With such developments, some analysts saw the EU as a potential developmental actor capable of shaping division-of-labour norms to ensure aid coordination among donors (Mürle 2007; Schulz 2007). Later studies, however, came to show that the EU has been an actor, especially in coming up with common initiatives in Brussels; however, on the ground where the aid is implemented, there is still a lack of coordination even among European donors (Carbone 2013:348; OECD-DAC 2012:76–79; O'Riordan et al 2011:112; Delputte and Orbie 2014). This situation is also expected to occur in the EAC, since there is no full integration of European initiatives. As a result, the EU is likely not to be considered as a coordinating actor in the region.

This section has explained how donor coordination will be analysed. Partial harmonisation mechanisms such as co-financing, lead donor initiatives and specialisation are expected to be used as means of donor coordination. On the other hand, as European regional aid is not fully integrated, this might have the negative effect on the EU of not being regarded as a coordinating actor in the region. The behaviour of the EU and its member states can lead to proliferation of donor activities, and thus cause various challenges to regional actors, especially when they have to engage with European initiatives in their different channels.

Donor Proliferation Analysis

Earlier in this chapter, I introduced a concept of donor proliferation to show how negative effects can occur when there is an increasing number of aid sources channelled via different delivery methods to recipients without proper coordination. As European donors support regional integration in the EAC via different channels, it can be expected that they use different aid delivery methods, thus causing different challenges to the EAC. This is experienced when each donor follows its own cycles of managing its aid projects. The EU aid project cycle, for instance, follows five different phases of managing aid, including programming, identification, formulation, implementation, and evaluation and audit (EuropeAID 2004:16). Such phases also exist in other donor initiatives and various challenges might occur when recipients have to engage with different development partners in each of these stages of their aid projects.

Studies have shown how various transaction costs of aid proliferation can be incurred by recipients, resulting from donors' engagement in multiple channels of providing assistance. According to Morss (1984:465), government officials in these recipient countries may be highly engaged in writing proposals to please different donor countries instead of working on their own national development goals. Furthermore, implementation of these different projects, and reporting systems to each donor, could even lead to unnecessary costs (ibid.). Such additional costs related to donor activities could have more meaningful impact if they were diverted to focus on real development in recipient countries. In addition to the high administrative burden and wasted resources, aid proliferation could also encourage corruption and slow economic growth in recipient countries (Knack and Rahman 2007). At the same time, donors have also been engaged in "poaching" qualified local labour, enticing people to work in their aid programmes (Aldasoro et al. 2010: 921).

To systematically analyse transaction costs, Acharya et al. (2006:6) divided them into two categories:

(a) direct transactions costs, that essentially take the form of the absorption of the scarce energies and attentions of relatively senior government staff; and (b) indirect transactions costs, that take the form of the dysfunctional bureaucratic and political behaviour that is stimulated by aid proliferation.

In this context, direct transaction costs occur if each donor requires separate rules of engagement in terms of negotiations, management and reporting requirements of their aid projects thus leading to "absorbing the energy and attention of (senior) politicians and bureaucrats to an inefficient degree" (ibid.). On the other hand, indirect transaction costs are those related to poaching of local bureaucrats, mismanagement of funds as well as competition and corruptions that can occur in connection to multiple aid projects (ibid.:7). In this book I will mainly explore direct transaction costs by assessing the perceptions of regional actors involved in regional aid as to whether they experience different challenges related to Europe's involvement in different channels. The analysis will mainly focus on three main stages of the aid cycle, including identification, implementation and reporting, which could require EAC bureaucrats to intensively work together with each donor in their different channels.

At the identification phase of the aid cycle, donors and recipients tend to figure out what projects and sectors could be supported within a specific aid budget. This phase typically requires several meetings between both sides to assess the relevance and likely feasibility of the project ideas intended to be supported. For EU aid projects, for instance, the purpose of identification also involves pinpointing project ideas that are consistent with the recipient and the EU's development priorities (EuropeAID 2004:27). EU member states can also have different development priorities they would like to link to their regional aid, thus making the identification process with the regional bureaucrats very cumbersome. If the EU and its member states follow different processes of identifying projects and sectors to be supported via regional aid, this would mean that the EAC bureaucrats would have to deal with different European initiatives separately. In that sense, complaints can be expected from EAC officials, especially if they need to invest a lot of time in identification phases with different regional donors.

The implementation phase is another critical stage of the aid cycle, whereby the planned benefits of aid projects are supposed to be delivered. It is also a stage in which the funds are made available to execute the projects; thus there are also concerns about how resources are managed throughout implementation of the activities. At this stage, donors might have different styles of implementing their aid based on their own rules and regulations of executing funds. In this way, if donors use different implementation strategies for their projects, it will also mean lots of work for the recipient to cope with each donor initiative. To avoid challenges related to different implementation strategies by donor countries, scholars propose that recipients should take leadership roles in coordinating donors in order to ensure aid effectiveness (Bandstein 2007:10; Foster and Leavy 2001:5; Brown et al 2001:7). In this sense, if the EAC does not practise a strong coordinating role and European initiatives pursue different implementation strategies in their promotion of regional integration, then complaints and criticism towards European regional aid can be expected.

Provision of reports to those providing financial resources is also an essential element of aid project cycles. At this stage, records are provided on what has been done and whether the objectives of financed projects have been reached. Reporting processes happen not only towards the end of aid projects, but there are instances whereby reports are required during different phases while the project is still ongoing. As mentioned earlier in this section, transaction costs within reporting can be incurred by recipient countries if bureaucrats have to provide separate reports to every donor engaged in financing different projects. Throughout reporting, bureaucrats may have to adjust the report style to fit donors' different requirements, for instance, in terms of their language and forms of expression, policy idioms and financial years (Acharya et al. 2006:6). Such challenges can also be experienced by EAC bureaucrats, especially if they have to separately report to the EU as well as to the member states in their different bilateral initiatives.

Different aid delivery methods that are used by European countries in their separate channels to promote regional integration are expected to cause various challenges to EAC bureaucrats. I have selected three stages of the project aid cycle (identification, implementation and reporting) to assess how regional actors experience challenges related to European regional aid. The aim is also to extend further the studies that have analysed donor proliferation but are mainly focused on recipient countries. Regional aid could also be affected by such challenges; thus, regional actors' experiences in engaging with donors in their different channels could provide new insights on donor proliferation.

Donor Coordination and Proliferation Analysis

This chapter has provided explanations about how I will analyse the effects of European initiatives in the EAC through assessing the degree of donor coordination and aid proliferation in the region. I have argued that European countries have not fully integrated their initiatives to support regional integration in the EAC; instead, they have likely adopted partial harmonisation mechanisms to coordinate their regional aid. It is this lack of full integration that is expected to lead to critical perceptions towards European regional aid. In that sense, the EU is expected not to be regarded as a coordinating actor in the region and critical perceptions are also expected from regional actors who have to engage with European donors' projects in their different aid modalities in terms of identification, implementation and reporting phases.

To answer the questions raised in this third part of the book, I rely heavily on the interviews. One of the key open-ended questions which I asked interviewees was to do with how they regard donor coordination on regional aid and whether the EU can be regarded as a coordinating actor, as argued in some literature. This was a question asked of all officials from the EU and its member states in the region as well as those from the EAC and partner states. There were other specific questions that I asked EAC and national officials regarding what they think about the fact that European countries support their integration process via the EU but also, at the same time, via different bilateral initiatives. In addition, a question connected to the challenges experienced by regional actors due to Europeans operating in different channels was also asked. Furthermore, to achieve a high degree of certainty, the responses provided by the interviewees are also triangulated to other primary and secondary data based on existing regional aid reports and programmes.

The assumptions made in this section can also be used to generally assess the effects of donor initiatives in other regional organisations beyond the EAC. If similar conditions of lacking full coordination by donor countries occur, then different challenges are expected to be incurred by bureaucrats in recipient regions. Furthermore, if the EU and its member states are all involved in financing similar projects, then the EU is likely not to be regarded as a coordinating actor in those specific regions. Now that I have explained how donor coordination and proliferation will be analysed, the following chapter moves on to explore the empirical situation on the ground.

7 Coordination and Proliferation on the Ground

We now come to the empirical part of analysing donor coordination and proliferation at the recipient level on the ground. Considering the numbers of donors involved in supporting the EAC, most of them are EU member states, and therefore European regional aid coordination could potentially reduce transaction costs associated with aid proliferation. As we will see, European countries have only partially coordinated their support to the EAC and that has presented various challenges to regional bureaucrats in engaging with the EU and its member states in their different channels. In this chapter, I start by elaborating how European initiatives are involved in supporting different regional sectors and projects. I will go on to assess how European regional aid is partially coordinated in the EAC. In this same section, I also evaluate whether the EU is perceived as an aid-coordinating actor in the region, as proposed in some literature. The third section deals with the perceived challenges experienced by regional actors due to the proliferation of initiatives by European countries, followed by a summary section of the lessons learned from the ground on regional aid.

Regional Sectors and Projects Support

As explained in earlier chapters, European countries employ four different main channels in their support to the EAC: a multilateral institution, the Partnership Fund, a non-profit company and bilateral institutions. Through the multilateral institution, countries contribute to the European Development Fund – finances used by the EU to support, among other things, regional integration. The Partnership Fund involves contributions by donor countries to a basket fund that supports EAC integration projects. Other donors use a non-profit company, TMEA, whereas Germany decided to use its bilateral institutions to support integration. Through all these channels, various projects can be supported in five different sectors of regional integration, including regional economic integration, peace, institutions, non-state actors and member-state capacity-building. Table 7.1 shows that in all four channels used to support the EAC, all donor countries are financing projects in regional economic integration as well as in regional institutions and non-state actors.

DOI: 10.4324/9781003290155-10

Table 7.1 Support of Regional Integration in Different Sectors

Sectors	Multilateral Institution	Partnership Fund	Non-Profit Company	Bilateral Institution
Regional Economic Integration	1	1	1	1
Regional Peace	1	0	0	1
Regional Institutions	1	1	1	1
Regional Non-State Actors	1	1	1	1
Member-State Capacity-Building	0	0	1	0

Source: Author's Own Compilation

There are exemptions in the areas of regional peace and member-state capacity-building, whereby some donors do not finance projects in those sectors. In this section, we explore how these sectors are supported by European initiatives in their different channels.

Regional Economic Integration

Economic integration is one of the most common sectors donors prefer to support when they engage with the EAC. Funds allocated in this area can be aimed at facilitating trade as well as investments, not only within countries in the region but also with other nations beyond their borders. In all four channels to promote regional integration in the EAC, donors finance projects to foster regional economic integration. In the case of the EU, for instance, most of the funds which have been allocated to the EAC have been earmarked to economic integration–related projects. As shown in Chapter 3, in the 11th EDF budget from 2014 to 2020 the EU allocated EUR 85 million to the EAC for its integration process (Regional Indicative Programme for EA-SA-IO 2014–2020). Almost half of that amount, EUR 45 million, was channelled to regional economic integration activities (ibid.). Within that budget, EUR 35 million were targeted to facilitate trade, specifically for small and medium-sized enterprises, and the remaining EUR 10 million was aimed at supporting implementation of a common market and customs union (Interview with EU diplomat, Dar es Salaam, 24 April 2015).

In different bilateral channels to support the EAC, European donor countries are also financing economic integration projects. Through the EAC Partnership Fund, for instance, most of the finances were also earmarked for economic integration projects. In the last disbursement to the basket fund in the financial year 2014/2015, whereby an amount of USD 6.9 million was donated, the financial plan indicated that USD 3.7 million of that budget was allocated to the implementation of common market and customs union protocols, whereas USD 747,230 was earmarked to support single currency initiatives in the EAC through the implementation of the East African Monetary Union Protocol (EAC 2014).

Under the TMEA channel, the support of regional economic integration plays a special role in their initiative. During the first phase of the TMEA programme from 2010 to 2017, most of the financed activities were in the realm of economic integration. One of the major projects in this area was called One Stop Border Posts (OSBP) that helps to reduce time taken for people and goods to cross the borders. The OSBP aims at coordinating all inspection processes in the key borders of the region at one point (TMEA Annual Report 2014–2015). The border posts are also accompanied by a project on Integrated Border Management (IBM) which aims at getting the border agencies from different EAC countries to work together at their shared border post. Within the framework of regional economic integration, the TMEA also supports the elimination of non-tariff barriers (NTB) in border points by financing report centres for assessing NTB-related issues in the region. Furthermore, ports within the EAC partner states, including Dar es Salaam and Mombasa in Tanzania and Kenya respectively, are being funded by TMEA to boost their capacities to serve other landlocked countries in the region.

Through bilateral institutions, specifically Germany's usage of its national agency, the GIZ, projects related to regional economic integration have also been implemented. For example, in the third phase of the EAC-GIZ programme "Support to the EAC Integration Process" that began from 2013 to 2016, fostering economic integration in the EAC constituted, among other things, projects to promote tax harmonisation. The total budget of the third phase of the EAC-GIZ programme was EUR 16.6 million and a huge chunk of that amount was used to finance projects which were supposed to facilitate economic integration (GIZ, n.d). Promotion of tax harmonisation, for instance, mainly aimed at facilitating the realisation of the established common market in the EAC (Heidtmann et al. 2012:10). As shown in Chapter 5, Germany continues to finance economic integration activities in the EAC through a project called "Support to East African Market-Driven and People-Centred Integration," which is currently in its second phase, between 2022 and 2025.

Analysis of regional economic integration support shows that all channels are interested in financing the sector. Some of the projects within the EU multilateral channel, Partnership Fund and Germany's GIZ programme, focus on economic integration policies adopted by the EAC, mainly the customs union and common market as well as its plans to pursue a monetary union. Such similar projects could provide an opportunity for donors to coordinate themselves, rather than each of them engaging in their own initiatives. That has also been the main wish of the EAC, especially in the economic integration sector, where donors prefer to channel most of their finances. "Some of the projects are capital intensive that the partner states may find it so difficult to raise the money," emphasised an EAC official on why donor coordination is needed specifically in projects to support regional economic integration which require huge budgets (Interview with EAC official, Arusha, 8 May 2015).

Regional Peace

Regional peace is another important sector which is highly preferred by donors in their support of regional integration. In the context of the EAC, not all bilateral channels are involved in promoting regional peace; instead, it is mainly the EU and Germany's GIZ that have shown interest in the sector.[1] Within the EU's framework, from the budget of EUR 85 million which was allocated to the EAC during the 11th EDF from 2014 to 2020, an amount of EUR 15 million was earmarked to peace and security-related projects (Regional Indicative Programme for EA-SA-IO 2014–2020). The EU's support of peace and security in the EAC constituted projects such as promotion of democratic governance in the region; combatting terrorism, cross-border and transnational organised crime in terms of human trafficking and migrant smuggling; as well as trafficking of small arms and light weapons, wildlife and narcotics (ibid.).

Through Germany's national agency, GIZ, regional peace was supported through its own programme called the EAC-GIZ programme "Support to Peace and Security in the EAC" that operated from 2006 to 2014. One of the major focuses of the programme was to control the proliferation of small arms and light weapons. This was done through supporting the EAC's regional policy for arms control and management as well as providing direct support to partner states, for instance through enabling their initiatives for marking and registering weapons (GIZ 2011). In addition to this project, the GIZ programme went further to foster the peace and security department of the EAC Secretariat in establishing a Regional Early Warning Centre with a situation room for anticipating, monitoring and analysing conflicts within the region as well as in surrounding countries (EAC Germany 2016). In this programme, the aim was also to enable the secretariat to mediate regional conflicts and to coordinate and implement joint activities on peace and security with other regional and international organisations (ibid.). The GIZ programme, however, ended in 2014 due to changes of priorities in Germany's Ministry of Economic Cooperation and Development, whereby there were other new interests in supporting other sectors in the EAC beyond peace and security (Interview with German diplomat, Dar es Salaam, 27 April 2015; Interview with Germany's GIZ official, Arusha, 7 May 2015). As elaborated

---

1 Other EU member states do not support peace and security directly in the EAC. Most of them support peace and security through the AU. For example, Denmark, Finland, France, Germany, the Netherlands and Sweden support the East African Standby Force, which is one of the AU forces to support security in the region.

in Chapter 5, Germany is currently supporting peace and security within the EAC through an associated project at the AU level called the African Union Border Programme, which intends to mitigate cross-border security threats.

Analysis of regional peace shows that it is only Germany and the EU that are interested in this sector. In other channels, for instance, in the EAC Partnership Fund, no peace-related projects were financed. In the channel of TMEA, as we have seen in the previous section, the major focus is on trade and not on peace. As the EU and Germany are the only regional peace supporters, coordination of some of their projects could potentially be facilitated. As shown in focal areas, some of their interests are the same, for instance, in the project to control the proliferation of small arms and light weapons. The EU identified interests in dealing with trafficking of small arms and light weapons in its 11th EDF, whereas Germany's GIZ had already been involved in that area since the inception of its security policy programme in 2006.

Regional Institutions

Regional institutions are essential in implementing and facilitating integration processes, and as such, all channels engaged in supporting the EAC are involved in institutional capacity-building. To begin with the EU's support, the 11th EDF budget from 2014 to 2020 allocated EUR 5 million to enhance the capacity of the EAC Secretariat and other institutions to deliver effectively on their mandates (Regional Indicative Programme for EA-SA-IO 2014–2020). In addition to this, part of the funds allocated to regional economic integration was channelled to support the EAC Secretariat in monitoring the implementation of customs union and common market protocols (ibid.). Other EAC institutions that were supported were those dealing with the management of regional natural resources, such as the Lake Victoria Basin Commission (LVBC), which is mandated to coordinate sustainable development and management of the Lake Victoria Basin in the EAC partner states. In this case, EUR 20 million was allocated to support the integrated management and development of the shared water and fishery resources (ibid.).

Under the EAC Partnership Fund, institutional capacity-building was also highly supported by donor countries. Out of the USD 6.9 million allocated to the EAC during the last disbursement in financial year 2014/2015, part of it was earmarked to institutional capacity-building. The financial work plan for that year showed an amount of USD 2.7 million intended to finance capacity-strengthening of the EAC (EAC 2014). Some activities which were supported by the Partnership Fund under institutional capacity-building mainly involve training of EAC staff to effectively carry out their mandates, especially in the departments of human resources, finance, disaster and risk management as well as resource mobilisation (EAC Partnership Fund Annual Report FY 2013/14).

Within the framework of TMEA, institutional capacity-building has also been carried out by supporting EAC institutions. The TMEA office at the EAC's headquarters in Arusha is responsible for engaging with the three main coordinating organs of the EAC, including the secretariat, the parliament and the court. According to a TMEA official, the secretariat, which is the executive board of the EAC, is supported in its daily coordination task of integration, whereas the parliament is being fostered in their verification work of different activities, and the court typically receives training in order to gain the capacity to arbitrate and settle trade disputes (Interview with TMEA official, Arusha, 7 May 2015).

Through the bilateral engagement of Germany, via its national development agency, the GIZ, there is also a strong focus on supporting EAC institutional capacity-building. Already in the first phase of the EAC-GIZ programme "Support to the EAC Integration Process," which started in 2007, there has been a strong focus on strengthening mainly the EAC Secretariat in designing economic, social and political policies (Höcker 2008:10). Support to the secretariat has continued in the current programmes and other financial assistance towards other EAC organs has been provided by Germany. For instance, Germany's financial assistance of EUR 14 million for the construction of the EAC headquarters was intended to ensure all EAC organs, including the secretariat, the parliament and the court, are in the same building (BMZ 2011).

In this area of supporting regional institutions, almost all donors are interested in supporting the EAC's main three organs – the secretariat, the parliament and the court – to fulfil their regional mandates. In this sense, opportunities for donor coordination of their projects involving those organs could potentially be facilitated. However, as we will see, coordination between the EU and its member states remains partial, even in this sector.

Regional Non-state Actors

Supporting regional non-state actors in facilitating integration processes in the EAC is also a major focal area for most donor projects. All channels are involved in building capabilities of non-state actors to ensure that they fully participate in integration processes in the region. It is, however, important to emphasise that there are some projects analysed in other sectors, which could overlap with initiatives to support non-state actors. For instance, in the sector of regional economic integration, some donors also include projects to support non-state actors such as businesses and private sector enterprises to fully engage in economic activities at the regional level. An example of this can be found in the EU's initiatives to support non-state actors, which has been classified under promoting regional economic integration. Of the EUR 45 million earmarked to support economic integration, part has been allocated to the private sector to ensure that they highly engage in trade at the regional level (Regional Indicative Programme for EA-SA-IO 2014–2020).

The EAC Partnership Fund also had some projects to support non-state actors in the region. Under the work plan for the financial year 2014/2015, a budget of USD 974,450 was allocated towards enhancing public awareness and popular participation in the EAC (EAC 2014). This can also be regarded as focusing on non-states actors, especially by facilitating EAC citizens and organisations to fully engage in the integration process. Some of the efforts that have been financed in this area include, among other things, publication of newspaper supplements, participation in national trade fairs and exhibitions, organising EAC media summits, distribution of promotional materials, organising EAC university student debates and so forth (EAC Partnership Fund Annual Report FY 2013/14).

The TMEA channel, like the EU, also supports non-state actors under the framework of promoting regional economic integration. Their focus is on the private sector and civil society being able to implement regional policies in their countries (Mwangi 2014). This is done within their strategic objective of improving business competitiveness. Various projects have been supported in this area: conducting research; provision of grants to groups such as farmers, transport and logistic companies to encourage innovation procedures; supporting professional platforms to lobby for their interests; capacity-building to civil society organisations to increase their participation in regional decision-making; and organising public–private dialogue on various trade-related issues in the region (TMEA Annual Report 2013/2014).

Germany is also involved in supporting non-state actors through its national bilateral agency. Already in the first phase of the EAC-GIZ programme in 2007, there was a strong focus on strengthening the advocacy competencies of regional business associations and enhancing dialogue between the regional representatives of civil society and the EAC Secretariat (Höcker 2008:10). Such support towards non-state actors also continued in later phases of the programmes (GIZ, n.d). Even in Germany's EAC-GIZ programme on "Support to Peace and Security in the EAC," there was a project aimed at including non-state actors in peace and security initiatives in the region. This project facilitated a dialogue on peace and security within the region among different groups, involving government officials, civil society actors and EAC institutions (EAC Germany 2016). Furthermore, in the current GIZ project called "Digital Skills for an Innovative East African Industry," which began its current phase in 2021 and will end in 2024, the support is mainly targeted towards non-state actors, especially those in the private sector and entrepreneurs, in facilitating regional digital innovation.

Support of regional non-state actors is a sector that all channels to promote integration are engaged in, but this is done through different approaches and in different styles. Projects supported in this sector depend on how donors interpret the importance of non-state actors in facilitating integration in different areas. For some channels, for instance, through the EU and TMEA, support to non-state actors is highly linked to businesses and private sectors to actively engage in regional trade and investment. Through Germany's GIZ initiative there is not only a strong focus on businesses, but support is also geared towards actors involved in peace and security in the region. On the other hand, within the EAC Partnership Fund, a focus on non-state actors means involving citizens and organisations to participate in integration processes in the region. All these differences in approach and interpretation of support of non-state actors, even among European initiatives, could make donor coordination in this sector difficult.

Member-State Capacity-Building

Building capacity to EAC partner states in implementing their integration policies has been a major focus for TMEA through its different country offices in the region. The remaining three channels of supporting integration do not engage directly with member states in their regional policies. If the EU wants to engage with EAC countries directly, it does this via its national indicative programmes, signed with the countries themselves, which specialise mainly in regional projects. In this sense, while support of those specific countries towards integration can occur, those projects are regarded as aid towards individual recipient countries. This is also the case with Germany's bilateral initiative through the GIZ, which exclusively focuses on regional policies. When Germany wants to provide aid to specific countries, it can also do this through its bilateral national policy towards those nations. The EAC Partnership Fund also does not finance projects in member states, but its funds are exclusively used on EAC regional-level projects.

TMEA has a strong belief that "regional integration has to be implemented at the national level," so if different institutions in member states are not supported in executing regional policies, it will be hard to achieve integration goals (Interview with UK's DFID official, Dar es Salaam, 21 April 2015). Their model follows the principle of supporting integration at the regional and national level. They implement national-level projects through their offices in all EAC countries. In this context, they enable national institutions such as ministries, departments and agencies to execute regional policies in their countries. One of the major projects at the partner–state level is assisting in monitoring the progress of implementing the common market protocol through the East African Monitoring System (EAMS) (Interview with TMEA Official, Kampala, 25 May 2015). This is an online monitoring and evaluation management-information system used to monitor the implementation of the EAC Council and Summit decisions in partner states. In addition, TMEA also supports the National Bureau of Standards (NBS) in all countries to achieve regional harmonisation of standards and improve the quality of goods produced in the region (TMEA Annual Report 2014–2015). Even the structure of its aid itself allows donor countries to finance projects at regional and country levels. As we have seen in Chapter 5, Belgium used the opportunity to finance

TMEA's country-level projects in its former colonies of Rwanda and Burundi to facilitate their proper integration in the EAC.

Member-state support has been a typical area of TMEA due to its structure as a non-profit company that was able to establish offices in all countries. Some national bureaucrats in different EAC countries seem to like TMEA's approach because their departments and agencies also receive support from the company. In most of the interviews, national officials and bureaucrats explained how various projects are being implemented via TMEA through their national programmes. An official in Tanzania even called on other donors, especially the German bilateral initiative, to also coordinate some of its projects with TMEA, so as to also support capacity-building at the national level. According to her, at the national level is "where integration is taking place" (Interview with Tanzanian bureaucrat of the EAC Ministry, Dar es Salaam, 2 June 2015). Another Ugandan bureaucrat also emphasised this by calling on the EU to adopt projects to support member states in implementing their agreed integration goals (Interviews with Ugandan bureaucrat of the EAC Ministry, Kampala, 21 May 2015).

European Donor Coordination

The situation in the EAC clearly shows that European donors are supporting different sectors, and that, in some areas, they finance similar projects. Such duplication of efforts across regional projects raises concerns about whether there is European donor coordination in the region. In the current era of global commitment towards harmonisation, better coordination and efficient use of development assistance, the EU and its member states are also expected to coordinate their regional aid, at least partially. As we've seen in Chapter 6, the EU is also concerned with aid effectiveness, and it can be considered to be a potential actor when it comes to coordinating its member states, who have maintained their own bilateral development policies. In this section, I analyse European partial coordination mechanisms that have been employed in the EAC, and then assess actorness of the EU in coordinating its member states.

Partial Coordination Mechanisms

As explained in Chapter 6, the highest and most ambitious degree of aid coordination is when donors fully integrate their activities while supporting the recipients. In absence of that, development partners can also pursue partial harmonisation of their strategies and approaches when providing their aid. That has also been the EU's approach to coordinating its regional aid with those of its member states. To that end, three main partial coordination strategies that have been used include matching of projects; co-financing or provision of matching funds; and specialisation or leading donor approach.

Matching of projects as a means of partial coordination has mainly been employed by the EU in coordinating some of its support to sectors of regional economic integration and institutions. As we have seen in Table 7.1 on supporting regional integration, these are among the sectors in which all donor channels are involved, thus the possibility of project duplications and overlaps are likely to be experienced. In its support of regional economic integration and EAC institutions, the EU decided to match some of its projects with those supported via the EAC Partnership Fund. This became possible because the EU joined other donor countries in the EAC Partnership Fund as a non-contributing member. This meant that the EU did not contribute money directly to the fund, but it matched some of its activities with the projects supported via the Partnership Fund. In that way, the EU is regarded to have contributed "technically to the implementation of the activities of the Partnership Fund" (Interview with EU diplomat, Dar es Salaam, 24 April 2015). The reason the EU was unable to provide money directly to the Partnership Fund is because the EAC has not yet proved to have a sound financial management system (ibid.). On support to regional economic integration, for instance, the Partnership Fund agreement of the financial year 2014/2015 showed that the EU also coordinated some of its support with the fund and intended to finance economic integration–related activities with a budget of USD 2.3 million (EAC 2014). In the case of capacity-building of regional institutions, the EU planned to finance activities in this area with USD 657,770 (ibid.).

Co-financing or provision of matching funds has also been a strategy used by the EU to coordinate some of its regional support in the area of regional peace. In this context, the EU provided matching funds to Germany's GIZ peace and security programme, specifically in the component of controlling the proliferation of small arms and light weapons (GIZ 2012). As explained in the previous section, Germany's GIZ has had a programme with the EAC that supported projects on small arms and light weapons since 2006. By the same token, the EU's regional indicative programme also showed interest in supporting initiatives on small arms and light weapons. Since the GIZ programme had already established itself in that field, the EU provided matching funds to the project as a means of partly coordinating its regional peace support to the EAC. This also confirms the statement by a German official who used the example of peace and security to explain the existence of project coordination with the EU through "co-financing agreements" (Interview with German diplomat, Dar es Salaam, 27 April 2015). Furthermore, co-financing from the EU in Germany's GIZ activities has also occurred recently in the project "Support to East African Market-Driven and People-Centred Integration." As shown in Chapter 5, during the first phase of the project from 2019 to 2022, a budget of EUR 13.4 million was earmarked to finance its activities and out of that amount, EUR 10.6 million came from the German government, whereas EUR 2.8 million came from the EU. Additionally, the EU also joined TMEA as a donor and has co-financed some of the company's activities since the financial year 2017/2018 (TMEA Annual Report 2017–2018:13).

The specialisation, or leading donor, approach is also a strategy used by the EU through channelling some of its resources via Germany's programme on regional peace in the area of small arms and light weapons. In that sense, the EU recognised Germany as a leading donor in the field of regional peace and it did not see a need to establish a similar project in the same area. In an interview with the EU diplomat, he used the example of supporting regional peace as a strategy of the EU to coordinate with its member states: "If member states are strong in certain sectors, we give them money to implement some of our projects ... if the EU is strong in certain sectors they might also ask us to implement some of their budgets" (Interview with EU diplomat, Dar es Salaam, 24 April 2015). Germany has also been regarded as the oldest partner for the EAC around the issues of peace and security through its policy programme in this sector that started in 2006 and ended in 2014 (Interview with EAC official, Dar es Salaam, 30 April 2015). In this sense, the fact that the EU provided matching funds to the GIZ programme was a sign of recognition towards Germany as a leading donor in the area of peace and security. Even when Germany's programme ended in 2014, the EU continued to finance peace and security in the EAC through the EDF (ibid.).

The situation in the EAC shows that the EU partially coordinates some of its projects with those from the member states engaged in the channels of the EAC Partnership Fund and bilateral institutions pursued by Germany. Matching of projects has been used to coordinate some activities in supporting economic integration and regional institutions with those in the EAC Partnership Fund. Co-financing and specialisation have mainly been employed in coordinating with Germany's GIZ programme in the area of peace and security. Furthermore, the EU's membership in TMEA as a donor since the financial year 2017/2018 is also a recent example of pursuing co-financing and specialisation within different channels of supporting regional integration in the EAC.

Perceptions of EU Actorness

With such EU initiatives to partially coordinate some of its regional projects with those of the member states, the question of whether the EU can be perceived as a coordinating actor is of major concern in the literature. The EU, as a multilateral donor with capacity to provide aid, while its member states can also do the same through their bilateral initiatives, has been regarded as having the ability to coordinate its member states and shape global debates on donor coordination. The question then asked is whether the European officials themselves working in those aid programmes in the EAC, as well as local

EAC actors and national bureaucrats, consider the EU as a coordinating actor in the region.

All European officials in the EAC region who I interviewed seemed not to consider the EU as a coordinating actor when it comes to regional aid. Some of them even regarded member states as main coordinating actors rather than the EU when it comes to supporting the EAC. As we saw in Chapter 5, it was Germany and Norway that invented the EAC Partnership Fund that coordinated all the donor countries to put their finances in a basket when supporting the EAC. Even the EU itself, as explained earlier, joined the fund as a non-contributing member and started to match some of its projects with those supported through the fund. This shows that it is the EU that has been coordinated by its member states, rather than the other way around. The example of the EU co-financing projects on small arms and light weapons within the GIZ peace and security programme can also be regarded as a sign of how the EU can be coordinated by Germany, especially given the country's identity as an early supporter of integration in the EAC since 1999.

One of the issues that became clear in all the interviews with the European officials was the fact that when it comes to development aid, the EU follows what the member states want. The EU diplomat even emphasised this by explaining how the EDF money used by the EU to pay for regional projects is financed and managed by EU member states: "EDF money is managed by the partners; they decide what to do with the money. They also participate and put forward their ideas. It's the partners who come with the demands" (Interview with EU Diplomat, Dar es Salaam, 24 April 2015). Responses from European regional officials show clearly that it can be difficult for the EU to take the leading role as a coordinating actor when it comes to regional aid in the EAC.

EAC officials and national bureaucrats, on the other hand, understand why the EU and its member states are all involved in supporting regional integration without full integration of their initiatives. Most of them do not regard the EU as a coordinating actor and some of them see the institution as a tool for powerful member states to pursue their interests in the region (Interview with Rwandan bureaucrat of the Ministry of Finance, Kigali, 25 May 2015). Another bureaucrat even hinted that it is member states themselves who could hinder the EU in becoming a coordinating actor, because they also have their competing national interests towards the EAC countries which they would like to pursue through their bilateral initiatives (Interview with Rwandan bureaucrat of the EAC Ministry, Kigali, 27 May 2015). Lack of full harmonisation of European initiatives in supporting regional integration is one of the clear pieces of evidence mentioned by an EAC official for the lack of a donor coordinating actor when it comes to regional aid (Interview with EAC official, Arusha, 8 May 2015).

The perceptions of all the officials, both from European and EAC side in the region, show clearly that the EU is not regarded as a coordinating actor. Despite EU initiatives to partially coordinate some of its regional projects with those of its member states through matching of activities, co-financing and specialisation, this has not helped change the perceptions of regional actors. Member states, such as Germany, with long-time experience of the EAC, have been regarded as more likely potential actors than the EU itself when it comes to donor coordination in the region. In fact, the existence of member states' bilateral initiatives have contributed to negative perceptions of the EU, being considered as a coordinating actor in the region, as some of the bureaucrats have described.

Donor Proliferation Challenges

The fact that European countries have only partially coordinated their activities while still operating in their different channels is expected to have negative effects on the EAC associated with problems of donor proliferation. In this section, I respond to the question of whether there are challenges experienced by regional actors resulting from the lack of full European regional aid coordination. As clarified in Chapter 6, I use three major phases of aid project cycles, including identification, implementation and reporting, to assess whether EAC bureaucrats experience different transaction costs when engaging with donors in their different aid delivery methods.

Identification of Projects

Because the EU and its member states operate in different channels to support regional integration, the EAC has to be involved in each of the identification phases of their projects. That is where the challenge is expected to occur, especially if EAC bureaucrats have to deal separately with each of those different initiatives in identifying projects and areas of regional assistance. Giving an example of an identification phase within EU projects, an EAC official explained that the EU would first and foremost identify its strategic interests and areas of concerns in the region. Those concerns might also be of strategic importance to the EAC; thus, the bloc would try to align its policy needs with those described by the EU. "They will give you the broad areas of which they can support which means you have to remain within the confines of those areas, and you cannot create your own areas" (Interview with EAC official, Dar es Salaam, 30 April 2015).

Within the framework of Germany's support to the EAC via the GIZ, the identification phase also involves, first and foremost, identification of focal areas with the involvement of different brainstorming meetings with the EAC bureaucrats. Germany's aid assistance would typically start at the parliament level, whereby the focal areas of development cooperation and the budget would be identified and earmarked. This would be followed by bilateral consultations between German bureaucrats and those from the recipient countries in order to identify areas of cooperation and projects to be supported. According to a GIZ official, "the negotiations with the EAC to identify areas of cooperation would take almost a year and would end up with signing of a protocol of cooperation that both sides would commit themselves to it" (Interview with GIZ official, Arusha, 7 May 2015).

In the channels to support the EAC through TMEA and the Partnership Fund, project identification procedures are different, since they involve different donor countries operating as a group. Through TMEA, individual donor countries can identify their areas of interest at country and regional levels and earmark their finances in those specific programmes in order for the company to implement those projects on their behalf (Interview with UK's DFID official, Dar es Salaam, 21 April 2015). The TMEA office in Arusha, at the EAC's headquarters, would engage directly with the EAC when identifying their regional projects (Interview with TMEA official, Arusha, 7 May 2015). Through the EAC Partnership Fund, since the money was going directly to the EAC, donors would identify the areas to be financed as a group together with the EAC, and the bloc would then receive the money to finance different integration projects.

The identification phase shows that the EAC has to engage with different donors in their separate channels in order to identify integration projects that could be financed via their development budgets. Part of the work for EAC bureaucrats is to merge donors' interests and their agenda on development cooperation towards the region with the needs of the EAC while identifying and confirming potential integration projects. If all donors coordinated themselves as one, or at least if the EU and its member states did that, then it would mean that EAC bureaucrats would have to engage with them just once when identifying those projects. Another additional challenge that EAC officials face during the identification phase is the fact that they have to develop so many interesting project ideas that can appeal to donor countries in their different channels (Interview with EAC official, Arusha, 8 May 2015. This, according to a TMEA local official from the region, makes supporting regional integration a donor-driven agenda "because each of those donors want to pursue their own strategic interests ... thus for the EAC as a bloc, it will not focus on what it really wants to do; it's being pulled every direction by these different donors who are coming with funding" (Interview with TMEA official, Arusha, 7 May 2015).

Implementation of Projects

When funds are made available to implement different regional integration projects, EAC bureaucrats also have to keep tracking all donor activities through their different initiatives. In all four channels used by European countries, implementation strategies are different. Through the EU's multilateral channel, for instance, the EAC would not receive funds to implement projects on their own, but the EU would directly finance projects that have been agreed in their cooperation contract. Within the channels of the non-profit company and use of national bilateral institutions, it is TMEA and GIZ respectively which are responsible for implementing regional projects. It is only through the EAC Partnership Fund that the EAC oversees implementation itself.

EAC officials complain about such multiplicity of implementing actors when it comes to regional projects. "It might be a challenge to know who is doing what and to what extent, so that the bloc can better manage policies and strategies to coordinate different projects in its regional integration processes" (Interview with EAC official, Arusha, 8 May 2015). The EAC wishes that all donors would simply give them their financial support directly and let the organisation coordinate and implement all the projects in different sectors (Interview with Germany's GIZ official, Arusha, 7 May 2015). In this case, the bloc could have a better overview of what is being done in different sectors of their regional integration process. Other national bureaucrats propose an alternative system called "joint aid assistance" in which donors are supposed to implement their projects in specific defined sectors under the supervision of the EAC (Interview with Kenyan bureaucrat of the EAC Ministry, Nairobi, 12 May 2015). On the other hand, development partners are sceptical about providing huge amounts of money directly to the EAC to implement projects on their own. As we saw in Chapter 5, donors were concerned about the EAC's mismanagement of the Partnership Fund and, starting in 2016, they stopped contributing to it and preferred to finance projects directly.

The question of donors implementing projects in different sectors raises different opinions from the EAC's side as well as on the side of European officials in the region. The former wishes that they could get all the finances and implement all donor projects, whereas the latter lack trust in the EAC's ability to manage funds. As implementation of most of the projects is not in the hands of the recipient, there are complaints that sometimes donors finance activities in partner states, for instance, projects related to standard-gauge railways connecting different countries, which, in the EAC's agenda, are regarded as regional projects. "What we always tell donors is that when you start implementing such a huge regional project, involve us so that we update our information and our statistics that our neighbouring countries should be able to know," emphasised an EAC official (Interview with EAC official, Arusha, 8 May 2015).

Reporting of Projects

Providing reports to different donors on how their finances have been used and whether the objectives of projects have been met can be a huge challenge facing bureaucrats. In the case of regional aid to the EAC, however, since in most of the channels donors manage finances on their own, reporting is mainly done by the donors themselves. As we saw earlier, development partners are sceptical about providing money directly to the EAC to implement projects on their own; therefore, they would directly pay for activities and produce their own reports. In this sense, transaction costs can only be incurred by bureaucrats when the EAC receives funds directly from donors, thereby needing each of them to be provided with reports.

In explaining how reporting with different donors is carried out, an EAC official stated that,

> it depends on how we signed the MoU, for example, with the EU we need to report to them directly, but there is one report done by the EAC called the EAC annual report which will show everything that the EAC has done, which all of them get. If donors gave the money for a certain project, we report to them differently.
>
> (Interview with EAC official, Arusha,
> 7 May 2015)

In most of the cases, however, donors write their own reports. For instance, through the TMEA channel, reporting of their projects is done directly by their offices at country and regional levels (Interview with UK's DFID official, Dar es Salaam, 21 April 2015). In Germany's bilateral initiative as well, the GIZ would have its own private mechanisms to report on its funded activities (Interview with Germany's GIZ official, Arusha, 7 May 2015). Through the EAC Partnership Fund, whereby the EAC receives funds directly from donors, EAC bureaucrats would prepare only one report on financed activities and give it to all the donor members participating in the fund. "We do not mention to each and every donor on what their money paid for in Partnership Fund activities, but rather we show what the fund financed in general and give one report to all of them," an EAC official clarified (Interview with EAC official, Arusha, 7 May 2015).

Because in some situations donors report on their own projects, this becomes a challenge for EAC bureaucrats to assess exactly what has been achieved through regional aid. A case in point is the EAC parliament, the EALA. One of its functions is to scrutinise and control spending of the EAC activities; their work becomes difficult especially when donors' finances do not go through EAC budget procedures. According to an EAC official, when donors finance projects and report on their own, it becomes challenging to be controlled by the parliament (Interview with EAC official, Arusha, 8 May 2015). Donors also understand this challenge facing the parliament, as stated by a German diplomat, "it's very difficult for EALA to understand what the resources are that go to the EAC and have the Secretary General held accountable for, because they are not on the budget" (Interview with German diplomat, Dar es Salaam, 27 April 2015). Some national bureaucrats, on the other hand, are critical of leaving donors to finance any projects they want and do reporting on their own. Donors could spend a lot of money on different issues such as consultancies as well as sponsoring various workshops, but it might be difficult to "quantify how they impact integration" (Interview with Kenyan bureaucrat of the EAC Ministry, Nairobi, 12 May 2015). In this sense, if donor countries do not provide the EAC their finances so that it can be budgeted, but instead pay for everything on their own, then "it's hard to control the value of the money they spend on regional integration" (ibid.).

Perceptions on reporting of projects show clearly that it might not be a huge challenge for EAC bureaucrats, specifically if donors prefer to finance activities and report on their own. This spares the EAC from producing reports to donors in their different channels, especially if they have not directly received the finances. Even in the case when a group of donors provide funds to the EAC, the bloc can produce one report to all of them. On the other hand, challenges occur when the EAC has to scrutinise and control the finances which have been spent by donor countries. For the parliament, this proves difficult because these finances are not budgeted within the EAC framework. At the same time, questions regarding donor self-reporting also arise as to whether those projects supported by them are really having major impacts on the EAC integration process.

Lessons from the Ground

In a statement that signalled discontent with donor proliferation and the various challenges to local bureaucrats, an EAC official stated that "the issue of donor dependence is big. In our budget about 65% is donor dependent which is not good, but most of the areas of support are capital intensive, for example the roads and railways" (Interview with EAC official, Arusha, 8 May 2015). Such dependency provides leverage to donors to come to the region and decide to engage in different projects, and as such, most of the time they implement these projects themselves through their own channels. This is why a local expert criticised the relations between European countries and the EAC as "not a win–win situation but rather win–lose situation … It's a political mathematics pretending that we want to elevate them so that we can term them economically and make them not think about sources of funding" (Interview with EAC expert, Arusha, 8 May 2015).

Even with such challenges as donor dependency, donors are expected to coordinate their initiatives to ensure aid effectiveness. The ideal scenario in this context is full integration of their activities; however, as we have seen in this chapter, European countries have only partially harmonised their support to the EAC. The EU has mainly used strategies including matching of projects, co-financing and specialisation to partially coordinate some of its projects with those of its member states in their different channels. That has been the case in sectors of regional economic integration and capacity-building to regional institutions, whereby the strategy of matching activities has been used by the EU to coordinate projects with the EAC Partnership Fund, whereas co-financing and specialisation have mainly been employed by the EU in conjunction with Germany's GIZ programme of fostering regional peace and economic integration and through participating in some of TMEA's activities. Despite such initiatives, the EU has not been regarded as a coordinating actor in the region, as some literature has anticipated. Both European officials as well as those local EAC and national bureaucrats consider the EU to be an institution used by member states to pursue their own interests and concerns in the region in addition to their own bilateral initiatives.

As donor coordination is only partial, various challenges related to donor proliferation are also experienced by EAC regional actors through engaging with European initiatives in their different aid delivery methods. For instance, during the identification phases, they have to interact with all the donors and merge their interests with those of the EAC while identifying projects to be supported in different sectors. The implementation phase has also been described as challenging, especially when every donor implements its own project; it thereby becomes difficult for the EAC to have a clear overview on what is being done by each donor in connection with its general regional objectives. In the reporting phase, since most of the donors implement their own projects, they also do reporting on their own, except in situations where the EAC receives the funds to manage specific projects. However, concerns over reporting have been raised especially when bureaucrats would like to control the impact of donor finances that do not go via EAC budget procedures.

Empirical findings in this chapter show that regional aid, just like classical aid towards recipient countries, can also undergo challenges related to donor coordination and proliferation. Lacking coordination could even be more complicated at the regional level, since most of the supported projects, even within partner states, have to be linked to general goals of the regional organisation. It is the work of regional bureaucrats to ensure that whatever donors are doing fits in with regional plans. In this way, recipient regional organisations can experience transaction costs when donors' projects proliferate. The case of the EAC shows that the EU and its member states can also contribute to donor proliferation challenges due to their engagement in promoting regionalism in different channels and without full integration of their regional aid.

8 Conclusion

This book intended to cover the literature gap existing in the analyses of the EU's promotion of regional integration in other parts of the world. Most of the existing studies have focused on the EU but less on the initiatives of its member states in their bilateral support of regionalism. To that end, three major questions have been raised: (i) why do states promote regional integration multilaterally if they would rather do so bilaterally? (ii) Why do states choose different bilateral channels? And (iii) what are the effects of such differentiated European initiatives in the EAC? To respond to them, the book has been divided into three parts based on these questions, each starting with a chapter on the theoretical framework, followed by empirical evidence.

Regarding the question on multilateral promotion of regional integration, this study has employed a modified intergovernmentalism approach in combination with the theory of path dependence to show how development policy has been coordinated at the EU level over time, thus making it difficult for states to reject it even when they are interested in using other bilateral channels. Tracing the European development policy since 1957 through to recent times, the book shows how states' preferences towards the ACP countries differed over time, leading to a situation whereby common EU decisions did not satisfy all countries. In coordinating the three areas of cooperation – aid, trade and political dialogue – powerful states have been shown to have taken different positions based on their colonial ties with ACP countries. States in the "regionalist" camp preferred the European common development policy to focus on their former colonies, whereas those in the "globalist" camp emphasised concentrating on poor countries in general. Such differences led states to employ various bargaining techniques, such as compromises, concessions as well as engaging in issue linkages and side payments. As a result, the final outcomes of different phases of European common development policy towards ACP countries were not satisfactory to all member states. However, given the difficulties of rejecting policies that have been adopted in the past and over a long period of time (path dependence), the EU member states have to continue supporting regional integration multilaterally despite their interests in using other bilateral channels. It is argued further that through a multilateral approach, states can pursue common European interests, whereas via

DOI: 10.4324/9781003290155-11

their own bilateral initiatives they can secure their individual national preferences towards a targeted region.

In explaining states' choices as to using bilateral institutions, a non-profit company (TMEA) or contributing to the EAC Partnership Fund, three foreign policy analysis approaches based on power, interests and norms/identity have been employed. In analysing the outcome, the study considers a norm/identity-based approach to explain the actual cause of states' decisions. It is those ideational goals of norms and identity that influenced states' choices, especially on how they regard a specific bilateral channel as the best way of supporting integration and at the same time pursuing their interests. Germany, for instance, has been shown to have internalised the norm of regionalism promotion based on its own national experiences, and it also intends to preserve a unique identity as an old partner of the EAC, which is why it decided to engage with the bloc via its bilateral institutions. Other powerful countries with the ability to employ their national development agencies, such as France and the UK, do not seek this unique identity in the EAC, thus they can rely mainly on TMEA in their regionalism support. In fact, all donors using TMEA, whether powerful or small countries, regard doing so via the company as the best and most appropriate way of supporting regional economic integration in the EAC. Regarding donors' contributions to the EAC Partnership Fund, it has been argued that they donated to the basket fund in order to signal that they are concerned with the norm of donor coordination at the recipient level. That is why the Partnership Fund became an additional possibility for donors to engage with the EAC beyond their other bilateral channels of interest. While the norm/identity-based approach is regarded as determining actual reasons for how states chose their bilateral strategies, the power-based approach is considered a sufficient condition in explaining the choices of powerful member states. This is based mainly on the capacities of influential countries and their colonial ties with the EAC partner states. It has been argued that Germany, which lost its colonies in the East African region, might be interested in reactivating a partnership with the EAC and therefore chose to do so with its bilateral institutions; whereas the UK, which had many colonies in other parts of Africa, or France, which had no direct colonial ties with the EAC countries, decided to mainly rely on TMEA. The interest-based approach, on the other hand, could not explain states' choices of bilateral channels since trade earnings between EAC countries and EU member states are rather low as compared to other countries like Nigeria and South Africa. As such, economic interests are regarded as future gains when EAC integration flourishes and is able to offer potential markets and areas of investment for those EU donor countries. In that regard, the future prospect argument even further strengthened the norm/identity-based approach that emphasises the importance of ideational goals, including what countries might perceive as future economic gains.

Analysis of the effects of European initiatives in the EAC involved development aid literature to determine the challenges that might be experienced in the region. In this sense, European donor coordination has been regarded as being partially harmonised since states operate in different multilateral and bilateral channels. This has been demonstrated to cause various challenges for EAC bureaucrats as they have to separately engage with the EU and its member states in their different stages of aid cycles including the identification, implementation and reporting phases. At the identification phase, bureaucrats have to interact with each donor when they intend to establish new projects. In this phase, they have to consider the EAC's regional interests but also the preferences of donors in the region. The implementation phase can also be challenging, especially if donors want to execute projects on their own and avoid delegating their aid to the EAC. In this context, bureaucrats complained that they sometimes lack a clear overview of different donor's projects and how their initiatives can be connected to the larger goal of the EAC. Similarly, during the reporting phase, donors could execute their own projects and decide to do their own reports, thus making it difficult for bureaucrats to control the real impact of their aid in the region. Lacking full coordination of these European initiatives has also been shown to affect the EU as it is not regarded as a coordinating actor in the region, despite its initiatives to engage in various forms of partial harmonisation through co-financing and matching of its projects with those of its member states.

Research and Policy Implications

The major research implication of this study is that European countries are also interested in supporting regional integration, and their bilateral actions, in addition to those multilateral initiatives at the EU level, can cause challenges to recipient regional organisations. This main finding contributes to the regionalism promotion literature that has focused mainly on the EU without paying much attention to the role of member states in doing the same (Börzel and Risse 2009, 2012; Lenz and Burilkov 2016; Farrell 2007). The case of the EAC shows that states can employ various bilateral channels, such as engaging independently with the bloc through their own national development agencies or in partnership with other donor countries, as in the case of using a non-profit company and contributing to the Partnership Fund. Such involvement of states has been shown to have negative consequences on the EU itself as it is not perceived as a coordinating actor in the East African region. This confirms other studies that have described how the EU can be actively engaged in donor coordination initiatives at international level as well as through establishing common development aid strategies; however, the reality on the ground where aid is delivered shows continual lack of coordination among European donors (Carbone 2013:348; OECD-DAC 2012:76–79; O'Riordan et al. 2011:112; Delputte and Orbie 2014). The focus on EU member states also confirms the findings of other foreign policy research that explicate how countries can engage with regional institutions to pursue their national interests, such as security and economic goals (Acharya 2001; Gruber 2000; Coleman 2007; Antkiewicz and Whalley 2005). This study describes further how states can pursue their national preferences through promoting regional integration via the EU by using aid, trade and political dialogue in combination with conditionality. Furthermore, they can also engage bilaterally with regional organisations to promote their individual national interests.

The findings are also consistent with the work of development aid researchers who have assessed the questions of donor coordination and aid proliferation (Acharya et al. 2006; Herman 2013; Knack et al. 2011; Klingebiel et al. 2017). Although most of them focus on classical aid to recipient countries, this study demonstrates that their analytical frameworks can also be applied to assess aid targeted to regional organisations. As in the case of recipient countries, similar channels of aid allocation can also be used in supporting regional integration. For example, the channelling of aid through NGOs used by donors to support the recipient countries (Nunnenkamp and Öhler 2011; Dreher et al. 2009; Nunnenkamp et al. 2009) can be seen as equivalent to allocation through the non-profit company in the case of the EAC. Also, states which are receiving aid normally have different ways of coordinating donor countries (Bigsten 2006); thus the EAC Partnership Fund could be seen as a strong example of this. Additionally, lacking full coordination has also been shown in this study to occur at the regional level; thus it is a challenge facing not only recipient countries. In this way, the findings of this book also contribute to current existing works that examine the impact of aid aimed towards regional organisations (Engel and Mattheis 2020; Söderbaum and Brolin 2016; Gray 2011; Jolliff 2015).

The result of this analysis also raises an interest in understanding further the driving factors of African regional integration processes. African countries have established several regional institutions from the continental one, the AU, to other subregional groups existing in different parts of the continent, such as the EAC. Most of the African countries even engage in multiple memberships in different regional organisations that have similar mandates. In the case of the old EAC member states, Tanzania, for instance, is also a member of SADC, whereas Kenya, Uganda, Rwanda and Burundi are also members of Common Market for Eastern and Southern Africa (COMESA). The question then becomes why African countries create many regional institutions but fail to contribute enough money to finance their integration activities. In explaining this puzzle, some scholars have suggested various alternative reasons beyond the usual suspects of achieving economic growth and regional security cooperation. The concept of "regime boosting" regionalism, for instance, has been used to show how some African leaders join regional institutions to increase government legitimacy through international summitry; thus their intention might not be implementing the mandates of these regional organisations but rather dealing with legitimacy problems (Söderbaum 2004;2016). External actors have also been regarded as major driving factors of African regionalism especially given the availability of external funding targeting integration activities, particularly in the areas of regional security (Engel and Porto 2010). Although African countries benefit from regional integration processes, for example in dealing with regional security challenges (Francis 2005, Iheduru 2011), this study indicates that questions of donor dependency and the influence of external actors remain relevant.

With regard to policy, it seems that regardless of the emphasis that has been directed towards African countries with regard to the importance of financing their integration processes, donor countries have continued to massively support regionalism in the continent. The case of the EAC shows that European countries can engage with recipients multilaterally via the EU as well as through their own bilateral channels. In this sense, full donor coordination should be encouraged in order to minimise the challenges faced by bureaucrats and also to ensure further effectiveness of regional aid. As donors have different interests, it is important that coordination is implemented by the recipients. The EAC Partnership Fund, which required donors to contribute their finances to the basket without earmarking them, was a good strategy to facilitate coordination at the recipient level. However, donors were sceptical of how the fund was being managed by the EAC, and they stopped contributing to it. In that regard, it is also important for bureaucrats to build more trust and show that they can handle the finances in a transparent and a meaningful way in order to facilitate coordination at the recipient level. In the long term, however, it is still important for African countries to reduce donor dependency if they want to have integration that fits their own needs and context. The EAC has very ambitious goals of achieving a monetary union and political unification; thus member states should also commit further to fully finance their regional integration activities.

References

Acharya, A. (2001). *Constructing a Security Community in Southeast Asia*. London: Routledge.

Acharya, A., de Lima, A.T.F. and Moore, M. (2006). Proliferation and Fragmentation: Transactions Costs and the Value of Aid. *The Journal of Development Studies*, 42(1), 1–21.

Adar, K.G. and Ngunyi, M. (1992). The Politics of Integration in East Africa Since Independence. In W.O Oyugi (Ed.), *Politics and Administration in East Africa*. Nairobi: Konrad Adenauer Foundation.

Adler, E. (2013). Constructivism in International Relations: Sources, Contributions, and Debates. In W. Carlsnaes, T. Risse and B.A. Simmons (Eds.), *Handbook of International Relations*. London: SAGE Publications Ltd.

AFD (2015). Assisting Regional Integration and Supporting the ECOWAS. Retrieved October 28, 2016, from http://www.afd.fr/lang/en/home/pays/afrique/geo-afr/nigeria/nigeria-ecowas

AFD (2021). The EU, Trademark East Africa and AFD Boost Regional Trade in the Horn of Africa. Retrieved November 25, 2022, from https://www.afd.fr/en/actualites/communique-de-presse/eu-trademark-east-africa-and-afd-boost-regional-trade-horn-africa

African Union (2022). African Union Border Programme (AUBP). Retrieved November 25, 2022, from https://www.peaceau.org/en/page/85-au-border-programme-aubp#:~:text=The%20African%20Union%20Border%20Programme%20offers%20a%20platform%20for%20the,integration%20through%20cross%20border%20cooperation

Aldasoro, I., Nunnenkamp, P. and Thiele, R. (2010). Less Aid Proliferation and More Donor Coordination? The Wide Gap Between Words and Deeds. *Journal of International Development* 22, 920–940.

Antkiewicz, A. and Whalley, J. (2005). China's New Regional Trade Agreement. *World Economy*, 28(10), 1539–1557.

Arts, K. and Byron, J. (1997). The Mid-term Review of the Lome IV Convention: Heralding the Future? *Third World Quarterly*, 18(1), 73–92.

Auswärtiges Amt (2015). Steinmeier Visits East African Community (EAC) Headquarters in Tanzania. Retrieved November 25, 2015, from http://www.auswaertiges-amt.de/EN/Mediathek/mediathek_video_node.html

Axelrod, R. and Keohane, R. (1986). Achieving Cooperation Under Anarchy: Strategies and Institutions, *World Politics*, 38(1), 226–254.

Axline, W.A. (1977). Underdevelopment, Dependence and Integration: The Politics of Regionalism in the Third World. *International Organization*, 31(1), 83–105.

Bagoyoko, N. and Gibert, M. (2009). The Linkage Between Security, Governance and Development: The European Union in Africa. *Journal of Development Studies*, 45(5), 789–814.

Bailey, R. (1983). *The European Connection. Implications of EEC Membership.* Oxford: Pergamon Press.

Balassa, B. (1973). *The Theory of Economic Integration.* London: Allen & Unwin.

Bandstein, S. (2007). *What Determines the Choice of Aid Modalities?: A Framework for Assessing Incentive Structures.* SADEV Report 2007: 4.

Bicchi, F. (2006). Our Size Fits All: Normative Power Europe and Mediterranean. *Journal of European Public Policy*, 13(2), 286–303.

Bigsten, A. (2006). Donor Coordination and the Uses of Aid. Göteborg University. Retrieved February 3, 2015, from http://gupea.ub.gu.se/dspace/bitstream/2077 /2723/1/gunwpe0196.pdf

BMZ (2011). Regional Cooperation in Africa. Germany's Contribution to Development. *GIZ Information Brochure 7/2011e.* Retrieved September 20, 2015, from https://www.bmz.de/en/publications/archiv/type_of_publication/ information_flyer/information_brochures/Materialie209_Information_Brochure _07_2011.pdf

Boekle, H., Rittberger, V. and Wagner, W. (2001). Constructive Foreign Policy Theory. In V. Rittberger (Ed.), *German Foreign Policy since Unification: Theories and Case Studies.* Manchester: Manchester University Press.

Börzel, T.A. and Risse, T. (2007). Europeanization: The Domestic Impact of European Union Politics. In: K.E. Jørgensen, M. Pollack and B. Rosamond (Eds.), *Handbook of European Union Politics.* London: Sage.

Börzel, T.A. and Risse, T. (2009). *Diffusing (Inter-) Regionalism: The EU as a Model of Regional Integration.* KFG Working Paper Series, Number 7. Berlin: Freie Universität Berlin.

Börzel, T.A. and Risse, T. (2012). From Europeanisation to Diffusion: Introduction. *West European Politics*, 35(1), 1–19.

Brown, A., Foster, M., Norton, A. and Naschold, F. (2001). The Status of Sector Wide Approaches, *ODI Working Paper 142*, January 2001, London: Overseas Development Institute.

Bruszt, L and Campos, NF (2019). Economic Integration and State Capacity. *Journal of Institutional Economics*, 15, 449–468.

Bundespräsidialamt (2015). Speech by Federal President Joachim Gauck to the East African Community During the State Visit to Tanzania 5 February 2015, Arusha. Retrieved November 25, 2015, from http://www.bundespraesident.de/SharedDocs /Downloads/DE/Reden/2015/02/150205-   Tansania-EAC-englisch.pdf;jsessionid =32EBBD7E0BA90D2D4797E73981DD0144.2_cid285?__blob=publicationFile

Burton, J. (1972). *World Society.* Cambridge: Cambridge University Press.

Carbone, M. (2007). Holding Europe Back: Italy and EU Development Policy. *Journal of Southern Europe and the Balkans*, 9(2), 169–182.

Carbone, M (2013). Between EU Actorness and Aid Effectiveness: The Logics of EU Aid to Sub-Saharan Africa. *International Relations*, 27(3), 341–355.

Clapham, C. (1996). *Africa and the International System: The Politics of State Survival.* Cambridge: Cambridge University Press.

Coleman, K.P. (2007). *International Organization and Peace Enforcement: The Politics of International Legitimacy.* Cambridge: Cambridge University Press.

Commission of the European Communities (1971). Commission Memorandum on a Community Development Co-operation Policy, Supplement 5/71: Annex to the Bulletin of the European Communities 9/10.

Commonwealth Secretariat (2004). *The Cotonou Agreement. A User's Guide*. London: Commonwealth Secretariat.

Council of the European Union (2003). A Secure Europe in a Better World: European Security Strategy. Retrieved November 24, 2022 from https://data.consilium.europa .eu/doc/document/ST-15895-2003-INIT/en/pdf

Cumming, G. (2013). UK-European Community Aid Relations Over the Lomé Years: Reciprocal Influences or a Dialogue de Sourds? In G. Bossuat and G.D. Cumming (Eds.), *France, Europe and Development Aid. From the Treaties of Rome to the Present Day*. Paris: IGPDE.

Delputte, S. and Orbie, J. (2014). The EU and Donor Coordination on the Ground: Perspectives from Tanzania and Zambia. *European Journal of Development Research*, 26, 676–691.

di Delupis, I.D. (1969). *The East African Community and the Common Market. The East African Community and Common Market*. Stockholm: PA Norstedt & Söners förlag.

Diez, T. (2005). Constructing the Self and Changing Others: Reconsidering 'Normative Power Europe'. *Millennium-Journal of International Studies*, 33(3), 613–636.

Dreher, A., Mölders, F. and Nunnenkamp, P. (2009). Aid Delivery Through Non-Governmental Organisations: Does the Aid Channel Matter for the Targeting of Swedish Aid? *The World Economy*, 33(2), 147–176.

Drieghe, L. and Orbie, J. (2009). Revolution in Times of Eurosclerosis: The Case of the First Lomé Convention. *L'Europe en Formation*, 3, 167–181.

Duchene, F. (1972). Europe's Role in World Peace. In R. Mayne (Ed.), *Europe Tomorrow: Sixteen Europeans Look Ahead*. London: Fontana.

Dür, A. (2011). Discriminating Among Rival Explanation: Some Tools for Small-n Researches. In T. Gschwend and F. Schimmelfennig (Eds.), *Research Design in Political Science: How to Practice What They Teach*. London: Palgrave Macmillan.

EAC (2013a). *Memorandum of Understanding between the East African Community and the Development Partners on the EAC Partnership Fund*. Arusha, Tanzania.

EAC (2013b). Protocol on Peace and Security. Retrieved from http://repository.eac .int/bitstream/handle/11671/1639/EAC%20PROTOCOL%20ON%20PEACE %20AND%20SECURITY.pdf?sequence=1&isAllowed=y

EAC (2014). Minutes of the 20th Partnership Fund Steering Committee Held at EAC Headquarters, Arusha, Tanzania.

EAC (2016). 4th EAC Partnership Fund High-level Dialogue Held in Dar. Retrieved November 17, 2016 from http://www.eac.int/news-and-media/press-releases /20160325/4th-eac-partnership-fund-high-level-dialogue-held-dar

EAC (2021). Communique of the 21st Ordinary Summit of the East African Community Heads of State. Retrieved November 24, 2022 from https://www.eac .int/communique/1942-communiqu%C3%A9-of-the-21st-ordinary-summit-of-the -east-african-community-heads-of-state

EAC (2022a). EAC Secretary General Hails the European Union for Lifting Financial Sanctions on the Republic of Burundi. Retrieved November 24, 2022 from https:// www.eac.int/press-releases/2368-eac-secretary-general-hails-the-european-union -for-lifting-financial-sanctions-on-the-republic-of-burundi

EAC (2022b). Partnership Fund. Retrieved November 28, 2022, from https://www.eac.int/terms/17-basic-page/431-640-654-partnership-fund

EAC (2022c). EAC Organs. Retrieved December 18, 2022, from https://www.eac.int/eac-organs

EAC Germany (2016). Promotion of Peace and Security in the East African Community. Retrieved March 15, 2016, from http://eacgermany.org/wp-content/uploads/2014/05/GIZ-EAC-Factsheet-P+S.pdf

EAC Germany (2022a). About German Development Cooperation. Retrieved November 26, 2022, from https://www.eacgermany.org/who-we-are/about-german-development-cooperation

EAC Germany (2022b). Peace & Security. Retrieved November 25, 2022, from https://www.eacgermany.org/sector/peace-security#trans

EAC Partnership Fund Annual Report for Financial Year 2013/14. EAC Headquarters, Arusha, Tanzania.

EAC-EU Press Release (2015). EAC-EU Political Dialogue: Arusha, 11 February 2015. Retrieved June 1, 2016 from http://eeas.europa.eu/delegations/tanzania/documents/press_corner/20150211_01_en.pdf

EAC Secretariat (2013). *East African Community Partnership Fund: Annual Report Financial Year 2011/2012*. Arusha, Tanzania.

EAC Update e-newsletter (2008). UK Backs Boost to Trade in East Africa. Issue Number 2008/20, 5 February 2008.

Elgström, O. (2006). Leader or Food-Dragger? Perceptions of the European Union in Multilateral International Negotiations. *Swedish Institute for European Policy Studies*, 2006, 1.

Engel, U. and Mattheis, F. (Eds.) (2020). *The Finances of Regional Organizations in the Global South. Follow the Money*. Oxon: Routledge.

Engel, U. and Porto, J.G. (Eds.) (2010). *Africa's New Peace and Security Architecture: Promoting Norms, Institutionalizing Solutions*. Farnham: Ashgate.

EuropeAID. (2004). *Aid Delivery Options Project Cycle Management (PCM) - Project Approach Guidelines, Project Cycle Management Guidelines* (Vol. 1, pp. 158). Brussels: EuropeAid Cooperation Office, European Commission.

European Commission (1975). *The Signing of the Lomé Convention: An Historic Event* (vol. 88/75). Brussels: Information Directorate-General. February 1975.

European Commission (1982). *The Community's Development Policy - Commission Memorandum, P-51, 30 September 1982, Brussels*.

European Commission (1996). *Green Paper on Relations Between the European Union and the ACP Countries on the Eve of the 21st Century: Challenges and Options for a New Partnership, 20 November 1996, COM(96)570 Final*, Brussels: Directorate-General VIII Development.

European Commission (2006). *Communication 'Strategy for Africa: An EU Regional Political Partnership for Peace, Security and Development in the Horn of Africa' COM (2006) 601 Final*. Brussels: European Commission.

European Commission (2014). Press Release: EU Strikes a Comprehensive Trade Deal With East African Community. Retrieved from http://europa.eu/rapid/press-release_IP-14-1170_en.htm

European Commission (2019). The Economic Impact of the EU: East African Community Economic Partnership Agreement. Retrieved November 16, 2019 from http://trade.ec.europa.eu/doclib/docs/2017/february/tradoc_155363.02%20Economic%20Impact%20of%20the%20EU%20-%20EAC%20EPA.pdf

European Commission (2022a). *Communication from the Commission to the European Parliament, the Council and the Court of Auditors: Annual Accounts of the European Development Fund 2021. COM(2022) 321 Final*, Brussels: European Commission.

European Commission (2022b). Economic Partnerships. Retrieved November 22, 2022 from https://policy.trade.ec.europa.eu/development-and-sustainability/economic-partnerships_en

European Council (1991). Presidency Conclusions. SN 151/3/91, 28 and 29 June 1991, Luxembourg: European Council.

.European Parliament (2022). Signature and Conclusion of the New Agreement between the EU and the Countries of Sub-Saharan Africa, the Caribbean and the Pacific (ACP-EU Post Cotonou. Retrieved November 17, 2022 from https://www.europarl.europa.eu/legislative-train/carriage/signature-of-the-new-eu-acp -agreement-(%E2%80%98-post-cotonou-%E2%80%98)/report?sid=6001

Farrell, M. (2007). From EU Model to External Policy? Promoting Regional Integration in the Rest of the World. In S. Meunier and K. McNamara (Eds.), *Making History: European Integration and Institutional Change*. Oxford: Oxford University Press.

Farrell, M. (2013). African Regionalism: External Influences and Continental Shaping Forces. In M. Carbone (Ed.), *The European Union in Africa: Incoherent Policies, Asymmetrical Partnership, Declining Relevance?* Manchester: Manchester University Press.

Federal Foreign Office (2011). Germany and Africa: A Strategy Paper by German Government. Retrieved July 10, 2016, from http://www.bmel.de/SharedDocs/Downloads/EN/International/Afrika-Konzept-EN.pdf;jsessionid=F1D37BB4004 9F75087304BE5ECDE02BF.2_cid358?__blob=publicationFile

Federal Foreign Office (2019). An Enhanced Partnership with Africa: Continuation and Further Development of the Federal Government's Africa Policy Guidelines. Retrieved November 26, 2022, from https://www.auswaertiges-amt.de/blob /2203542/6274c1b95ddfe1126f9d466a8d9e10c5/190327-afrika-ll-volltext-data.pdf

Finnemore, M. (1996). *National Interests in International Society*. Ithaca: Cornell University Press.

Forwood, G. (2001). The Road to Cotonou: Negotiating a Successor to Lomé. *JCMS: Journal of Common Market Studies*, 39(3), 423–442.

Foster, M. and Leavy, J. (2001). The Choice of Financial Aid Instruments, *ODI Working Paper*, 01 October 2001.

Francis, D.J. (2005). Expanding the Frontiers of Regional Integration: Regional Economic and Security Dynamics. In: R. Cline-Cole and E. Robson (Eds.), *West African Worlds: Paths Through Socio-Economic Change, Livelihoods and Development* (pp. 129–150). Harlow: Prentice-Hall.

French White Paper on Defence and National Security (2013). Ministère de la Défense/ SGA/SPAC.

Frisch, D. (2008). The European Union's Development Policy. *Policy Management Report*, 15.

Frisch, D. (2013). The Role of France and the French in European Development Cooperation Policy. In: G. Bossuat and G.D Cumming (Eds.), *France, Europe and Development Aid. From the Treaties of Rome to the Present Day*. Paris: IGPDE.

Gerring, J. and Seawright, J. (2007). *Case Study Research: Principles and Practices*. Cambridge: Cambridge University Press.

GIZ (2011). *EAC-GIZ Cooperation Towards East African Integration*. Arusha: GIZ GmbH.

GIZ (2012). Small Arms and Light Weapons in the East African Community. Impact Assessment of Control of Small Arms Between 2006 and 2012 Contributions by the GIZ Programme "Promotion of Peace and Security in the EAC". Retrieved from http://eacgermany.org/wp-content/uploads/2014/10/SALW-Summary -Report.jpg

GIZ (2016). Promotion of Peace and Security in the East African Community. Retrieved June 13, 2016, from http://eacgermany.org/wp-content/uploads/2014/05/GIZ-EAC -Factsheet-P+S.pdf

GIZ (2021). EAC-GIZ Overview. Retrieved November 27, 2022, from https://strapi .eacgermany.org/uploads/609d20536d58e589349173_cc446b2bef.pdf

GIZ (n.d.). *Cooperation East African Community Germany*. Arusha: GIZ.

Gray, J. (2011). External Actors and Outside Funding in South-South Regional Trade Agreements. Paper Presented at the Conference: The Political Economy of International Organizations, ETH Zurich, Switzerland.

Gruber, L. (2000). *Ruling the World: Power Politics and the Rise of Supranational Institutions*. Princeton: Princeton University Press.

Haas, E.B. 1964. *Beyond the National-State: Functionalism and International Organization*. Stanford, CA: Stanford University Press.

Hailey, N. (2015). Speech: Integrating East Africa: Progress, Challenges and Future Prospects. Retrieved June 12, 2015, from https://www.gov.uk/government/speeches /integrating-east-africa-progress-challenges-and-future-prospects

Hazlewood, A. (1985). The End of the East African Community: What are the Lessons for Regional Integration Schemes? In R.I Onwuka and A. Sesay (Eds.), *The Future of Regionalism in Africa*. New York: St. Martin's Press.

Heidtmann, M., Mueller, M. and Menning, B. (2012). *Towards the EAC Vision. EAC-GIZ Programme 'Support to the EAC Integration Process' Annual Report 2011*. Arusha: GIZ GmbH.

Herman, B. (2013). *Towards a New Global Partnership for Development: Looking Back to Look Forward. Background Study for DCF Ethiopia High-level Symposium; 5–7 June, Addis Ababa*. New York: ECOSOC.

Hewitt, A. (1991). Britain and the European Development Fund. In: A. Bose and P. Burnell (Eds.), *Britain's Overseas Aid Since 1979*. Manchester and New York: Manchester University Press.

HM Government (2015). *National Security Strategy and Strategic Defence and Security Review 2015: A Secure and Prosperous United Kingdom*, Cm 9161, Presented to Parliament by the Prime Minister by Command of Her Majesty, November 2015, London: Open Government Licence.

HM Treasury (2015). *UK Aid: Tackling Global Challenges in the National Interest*, Department for International Development, Cm 9163, Presented to Parliament by the Chancellor of the Exchequer by Command of Her Majesty, November 2015, London: Open Government Licence.

Höcker, U. (2008). *Supporting Regional Economic Integration and Cooperation*. Eschborn: GTZ GmbH. Retrieved September 15, 2015, from https://www.giz .de/fachexpertise/downloads/Fachexpertise/GTZ_2008_Supporting_Regional _Economic_Integration_and_Cooperation.pdf

Hoffmann, S. (1966). Obstinate or Obsolete? The Fate of the Nation-State and the Case of Western Europe. *Daedalus*, 95(3), 862–915.

Hugon, P. (2013). What Is Distinctive About European Development Aid? Taking Account of New Paradigms 1975–1995. In G. Bossuat and G.D Cumming (Eds.),

France, Europe and Development Aid. From the Treaties of Rome to the Present Day. Paris: IGPDE.

Hurrell, A. (1995). Explaining the Resurgence of Regionalism in World Politics. *Review of International Studies*, 21(4), 331–358.

Hurt, S.R. (2003). Co-operation and Coercion? The Cotonou Agreement Between the European Union and ACP States and the End of the Lomé Convention. *Third World Quarterly*, 24(1), 161–176.

Hurt, S.T. (2012). The EU-SADC Economic Partnership Agreement Negotiations: Locking in the Neoliberal Development Model in Southern Africa? *Third World Quarterly*, 33(3), 495–510.

Hyde-Price, A. (2006). 'Normative' Power Europe: A Realist Critique. *Journal of European Public Policy*, 13(2), 217–234.

Iheduru, O.C. (2011). The 'New' ECOWAS: Implications for the Study of Regional Integration. In T.M. Shaw, J.A. Grant and S. Cornelissen (Eds.), *The Ashgate Research Companion to Regionalism* (213–240). Farnham: Ashgate.

IMF Data on Direction of Trade Statistics (DOTS). Retrieved from http://data.imf.org/?sk=9D6028D4-F14A-464C-A2F2-59B2CD424B85&sId=1454703973993

Jolliff, B.J. (2015). Explaining A New Foreign Aid Recipient: The European Union's Provision of Aid to Regional Trade Agreements, 1995–2013. Paper Presented at the Conference: The Political Economy of International Organizations, University of Utah, USA.

Kant, I. (2006). *Towards Perpetual Peace and Other Writings on Politics, Peace and History*. New Haven: Yale University Press.

Keohane, R. and Nye, J.S. (1977). *Power and Interdependence: World Politics in Transition*. Boston: Little, Brown.

Klingebiel, S., Negre, M. and Morazán, P. (2017). Costs, Benefits and the Political Economy of Aid Coordination: The Case of the European Union. *European Journal of Development Research*, 29, 144–159.

Klotz, A. (1995). *Norms in International Relations: The Struggle Against Apartheid*, Ithaca: Cornell University Press.

Knack, S. and Rahman, A. (2004). Donor Fragmentation and Bureaucratic Quality in Aid Recipients. *World Bank Policy Research Working Paper 3186*, January 2004, Washington DC: World Bank.

Knack, S. and Rahman, A. (2007). Donor Fragmentation and Bureaucratic Quality in Aid Recipients. *Journal of Development Economics*, 83(1), 176–197.

Knack, S., Rogers, F.H. and Eubank, N. (2011). Aid Quality and Donor Rankings. *World Development*, 39(11), 1907–1917.

Langan, M. (2012). Normative Power Europe and the Moral Economy of Africa-EU Ties: A Conceptual Reorientation of 'Normative Power'. *New Political Economy*, 17(3), 243–270.

Lenz, T. and Burilkov, A. (2016). Institutional Pioneers in World Politics: Regional Institution Building and the Influence of the European Union. *European Journal of International Relations*. https://doi.org/10.1177/1354066116674261

Lenz, T., Bezuijen, J., Hooghe, L. and Marks, G. (2015). Patterns of International Organization: Task Specific vs. General Purpose. In E. da Conceicao-Heldt, M. Koch and A. Liese (Eds.), *International Organisationen. Politische Vierteljahresschrift, Sonderheft* (vol. 49, pp. 131–155). Baden-Baden: Nomos.

Libreville Declaration (1997). Retrieved from http://www.acp.int/content/libreville-declaration

Lindberg, L.N. 1970. Political Integration as a Multidimensional Phenomenon Requiring Multivariate Measurement. *International Organization*, 24(4), 649–731.

Lucarelli, S. and Manners, I. (2006). Valuing Principles in European Union Foreign Policy, In S. Lucarelli and I. Manners (Eds.), *Values and Principles in European Union Foreign Policy*. London and New York: Routledge.

Manners, I. (2002). Normative Power Europe: A Contradiction in Terms? *JCMS*, 40(2), 235–258.

Manners, I. and Whitman, R.G. (1998). Towards Identifying the International Identity of the European Union: A Framework for Analysis of the EU's Network of Relationship. *Journal of European Integration*, 21(3), 231–249.

Manners, I. and Whitman, R.G. (2003). The Difference Engine: Constructing and Representing the International Identity of the European Union. *Journal of European Public Policy*, 10(3), 380–404.

Mailafia, O. (1997). *Europe and Economic Reform in Africa. Structural Adjustment and Economic Diplomacy*. London and New York: Routledge.

Mayer, F.W. (1988). Bargains Within Bargains: Domestic Politics and International Negotiation. Diss, Harvard University.

Mearsheimer, J. (1994). The False Promise of International Institutions. *International Security*, 19(3), 4–49.

Migani, G. (2013). National Strategies and International Issues at the Inception of Community Development Aid: France, Sub-Saharan Africa and the Yaounde Convention. In: G. Bossuat and G.D. Cumming (Eds.), *France, Europe and Development Aid. From the Treaties of Rome to the Present Day*. Paris: IGPDE.

Milward, A.S. (1992). *The European Rescue of the Nation-State*. London: Routlege.

Ministry of Foreign Affairs of the Netherlands (2013). *A World to Gain: A New Agenda for Aid, Trade and Investment*. The Hague: Ministry of Foreign Affairs of the Netherlands.

Ministry of Foreign Affairs of the Netherlands (2022). *Do What We Do Best: A Strategy for Foreign Trade and Development Cooperation*. The Hague: Ministry of Foreign Affairs of the Netherlands.

Ministry of Foreign and European Affairs (2011). Strategy 2011: Development Cooperation: A French Vision. *Director-General of Global Affairs, Development and Partnerships*.

Mitrany, D. (1943). *A Working Peace System: An Argument for the Functional Development of International Organization*. London: Royal Institute of International Affairs.

Moravcsik, A. (1991). Negotiating the Single European Act: National Interests and Conventional Statecraft in the European Community, *International Organization*, 45(1), 19–56.

Moravcsik, A. (1993). Preferences and Power in the European Community: A Liberal Intergovernmentalist Approach. *Journal of Common Market Studies*, 31(4), 473–524

Moravcsik, A. (1995). Liberal Intergovernmentalism and Integration: A Rejoinder. *Journal of Common Market Studies*, 33(4), 611–628.

Moravcsik, A. (1998). *The Choice for Europe, Social Purpose & State Power from Messina to Maastricht*. Ithaca: Cornell University.

Morss, E.R. (1984). Institutional Destruction Resulting from Donor and Project Proliferation in Sub-Saharan African Countries. *World Development*, 12(4), 465–470.

Mürle, H. (2007). *Towards a Division of Labour in European Development Co-operation: Operational Options,* Discussion Paper, 6. Bonn: German Development Institute, June 2007.

Mwangi, E. (2014). Growing Prosperity Through Trade. Retrieved from http://www .cepal.org/sites/default/files/events/files/presentacion_elizabeth_mwangi_tmea.pdf

Mwilima, H.K. (2019). Brexit Linkage in Trade Negotiation: A Strategy for Rejecting the European Union: East African Community Economic Partnership Agreement? *L'Europe en formation*, 388, Spring–Summer 2019.

Negotiated Post-Cotonou Agreement (2021). Partnership Agreement between the European Union, the European Union and its Member States, of the One Part, and Members of the Organisation of African, Caribbean and Pacific States, of the Other Part. Retrieved November 20, 2022 from https://www.europarl.europa.eu/cmsdata /238376/Negotiated%20Agreement%20text%20initialled%20by%20the%20EU %20and%20OACPS%20chief%20negotiators%20on%2015th%20April%202021 .pdf

Nicolaidis, K. and Howse, R. (2002). This Is My EUtopia...: Narrative as Power. *JCMS*, 40(4), 767–792.

Nunnenkamp, P. and Öhler, H. (2011). Aid Allocation Through Various Official and Private Channels: Need, Merit and Self-Interest as Motives of German Donors. *World Bank*, 39(3), 308–323.

Nunnenkamp, P., Weingarth, J. and Weisser, J. (2009). Is NGO Aid Not So Different After All? Comparing the Allocation of Swiss Aid by Private and Official Donors. *European Journal of Political Economy*, 25(4), 422–438.

Nye, J.S. 1968. Comparative Regional Integration: Concept and Measurement. *International Organizations*, 22(4), 655–880.

OECD-DAC (2012). *European Union DAC Peer Review*. Paris: OECD-DAC.

O'Riordan, A., Benfield, A. and de Witte, E. (2011). *Joint Multi-Annual Programming*. Herts: HTSPE.

Orbie, J. and Carbone, M. (2016). The Europeanisation of Development Policy. *European Politics and Society*, 17(1), 1–11.

Parfitt, T.W. and Bullock, S. (1990). The Prospects for a New Lomé Convention: Structural Adjustment or Structural Transformation? *Review of African Political Economy*, 17(47), 104–116.

Powell, R. (1993). Absolute and Relative Gains in International Relations Theory. In D. Baldwin (Ed.), *Neorealism and Neoliberalism: The Contemporary Debate*. New York: Columbia University Press.

Posthumus, B. (1998). Beyond Lomé IV: Preliminary Views of European Governments on Future EU-ACP Relations. *ECDPM Working Papers 53,* 02 February 1998, Maastricht: ECDPM.

PTB (2022). East African Community: Strengthening the Regional Quality Infrastructure for Selected Sectors. Retrieved November 25, 2022, from https://www.ptb.de/cms/fileadmin/internet/fachabteilungen/abteilung_9/9.3 _internationale_zusammenarbeit/projektprofile/PTB_Project_EAC_95344_EN .pdf

Ravenhill, J. (1985). *Collective Clientelism. The Lomé Conventions and North-South Relations.* New York: Columbia University Press.

Regional Indicative Programme for EA-SA-IO (2014–2020). Retrieved from https://www.eeas.europa.eu/sites/default/files/rip-ea-sa-io-signed-20150604_en.pdf

Sandholtz, W. and Stone Sweet, A. (2013). Neo-Functionalism and Supranational Governance. In E. Jones, A. Menon and S. Weatherill (Eds.), *The Oxford Handbook of the European Union.* Oxford: Oxford University Press.

Scheipers, S. and Sicurelli, D. (2007). Normative Power Europe: A Credible Utopia? *JCMS*, 45(2), 435–457.

Schulz, N (2007). Division of Labour Among European Donors: Allotting the Pie or Committing to Effectiveness? *Development in Context*, 09 May 2007, p. 5.

Sebenius, J.K. (1983). Negotiation Arithmetic: Adding and Subtracting Issues and Parties. *International Organization*, 37(2), 281–316.

Solana, J. (n.d.). The Future of the European Union as an International Actor. Retrieved November 28, 2022, from https://www.consilium.europa.eu/uedocs/cms_data/docs/pressdata/en/articles/84349.pdf

Söderbaum, F. (2004). *The Political Economy of Regionalism. The Case of Southern Africa.* Basingstoke: Palgrave Macmillan.

Söderbaum, F. (2013). The European Union as an Actor in Africa: Internal Coherence and External Legitimacy. In M. Carbone (Ed.), *The European Union in Africa: Incoherent Policies, Asymmetrical Partnership, Declining Relevance?* Manchester: Manchester University Press.

Söderbaum, F. (2016). *Rethinking Regionalism.* New York: Palgrave Macmillan.

Söderbaum, F. and Brolin, T. (2016). Support to Regional Cooperation and Integration in Africa: What Works and Why? *Expertgruppen för bistandsanalys (EBA)*, Rapport 2016:01 till.

Storey, A. (2006). Normative Power Europe? Economic Partnership Agreements and Africa. *Journal of Contemporary African Studies*, 24(3), 331–346.

The Cotonou Agreement and Multiannual Financial Framework 2014–20. Retrieved from https://op.europa.eu/en/publication-detail/-/publication/c030c886-b15c-4456-930d-c9488db9cd0a

The Treaty for the Establishment of the East African Community, 30 November 1999 (entry into force 7 July 2000), EAC Publication 1.

TMEA Annual Repport 2013–2014. Retrieved November 25, 2022, from https://trademarkea.com/new-staging/wp-content/uploads/dlm_uploads/2015/03/TMEA-Annual-Report-2014-1.pdf

TMEA Annual Report 2014–2015. Retrieved November 25, 2022, from https://trademarkea.com/wp-content/uploads/dlm_uploads/2016/02/TMEA-Annual-Report-2014-15-1.pdf

TMEA Annual Report 2017–2018. Retrieved November 25, 2022, from https://trademarkea.com/wp-content/uploads/dlm_uploads/2019/03/TMEA-Annual-Report-20178-Final.pdf

TMEA Annual Report 2020–2021. Retrieved November 25, 2022, from https://www.trademarkea.com/wp-content/uploads/dlm_uploads/2022/03/AR-2020-2021-March-Final-1.pdf

Treaty Establishing the European Economic Community (Treaty of Rome), 25 March 1957, 294 U.N.T.S. 3 (entry into force 1 January 1958).

Treaty on European Union (Consolidated Version), Treaty of Maastricht, 7 February 1992, *Official Journal of the European Communities C*, 325/5, 24 December 2002.

Twitchett, C. (1978). *Europe and Africa: From Association to Partnership.* Westmead: Saxon House Limited.

UNCTAD II Conference (1968). Proceedings of the United Nations Conference on Trade and Development, Second Session, New Delhi, 1 February 29 March 1968, Volume 1, New York: United Nations.

van Zwanenberg, R.M.A. and King, A. (1975). *An Economic History of Kenya and Uganda, 1800–1970.* London: The Macmillan Press Ltd.

Wall, D. (1983). Britain, the EEC and the Third World. In R. Jenkins (Ed.), *Britain and the EEC.* London and Basingstoke: The Macmillan Press LTD.

Wallace, W. (1976). Atlantic Relations: Policy Co-ordination and Conflict. *International Affairs*, 52(2), 163–179.

Walt, S.M. (1995). Alliance Formation and the Balance of World Power. In M.E. Brown, S.M. Lynn-Jones and S.E. Miller (Eds.), *The Perils of Anarchy: Contemporary Realism and International Security.* Cambridge, MA: MIT Press.

Waltz, K. (1979). *Theory of International Politics.* Boston: McGraw-Hill.

Whittington, D. and Calhoun, C. (1988). Who Really Wants Donor Co-ordination? *Development Policy Review*, 6(3), 295–309.

World Bank (2013). Opening the Gates: How the Port of Dar es Salaam Can Transform Tanzania. *Tanzania Economic Update*, 3, 77729.

Yin, R.K. (2014). *Case Study Research: Design and Methods* (5th Ed). London: SAGE Publication, Inc.

Young, R. (2004). Normative Dynamics and Strategic Interests in the EU´s External Identity. *JCMS*, 42(2), 415–435.

Zartman, W. (1971). *The Politics of Trade Negotiations Between Africa and the European Economic Community. The Weak Confront the Strong.* Princeton: Princeton University Press.

Interviews

Belgian diplomat, 22 April 2015, in Dar es Salaam, Tanzania
Danish programme consultant, 7 May 2015, in Arusha, Tanzania
Danish programme official, 28 April 2015, in Dar es Salaam, Tanzania
EAC expert, 8 May 2015, in Arusha, Tanzania
EAC official, 30 April 2015, in Dar es Salaam, Tanzania
EAC official, 8 May 2015, in Arusha, Tanzania
EU diplomat, 24 April 2015, in Dar es Salaam, Tanzania
French diplomat, 9 June 2015, in Dar es Salaam, Tanzania
German diplomat, 27 April 2015, in Dar es Salaam, Tanzania
Germany's GIZ official, 7 May 2015, in Arusha, Tanzania
Kenyan bureaucrat of the EAC Ministry, 12 May 2015, in Nairobi, Kenya.
Rwandan bureaucrat of the Ministry of Finance, 25 May 2015, in Kigali, Rwanda
Rwandan bureaucrat of the EAC Ministry, 27 May 2015, in Kigali, Rwanda
Tanzanian bureaucrat at the EAC Ministry, 2 June 2015, in Dar es Salaam, Tanzania
TMEA official, 7 May 2015, in Arusha, Tanzania

TMEA Official, 25 May 2015, in Kampala, Uganda
Ugandan bureaucrat of the EAC Ministry, 21 May 2015, in Kampala, Uganda
UK's DFID official, 21 April 2015, in Dar es Salaam, Tanzania

Personal Communications

Dutch diplomat, 10 November 2015
EAC official, 11 November 2022
German diplomat, 10 November 2015
UK's DFID official, 28 August 2015

Index

Printed in the United States
by Baker & Taylor Publisher Services